AF616530

Picture Framing and Hanging

Also in the Tricks of the Trade Series

DECORATING
FLOORING
PLUMBING
ELECTRICAL WIRING
HOME CARPENTRY

Picture Framing and Hanging

Larry Blonstein

PELHAM BOOKS

First published in Great Britain by
Pelham Books Ltd
44 Bedford Square
London WC1B 3DU
1980

ISBN 0 7207 1242 4

Composition by Cambrian Typesetters and printed and bound in Great Britain by Redwood Burn Ltd, Trowbridge and Esher

Contents

Acknowledgements

My thanks are due first to Fred Keetch Ltd, picture framers, of Taunton, Somerset, from whom I learned many 'tricks of the trade'; to Frank B. Scragg & Co., of Birmingham, who keep the trade supplied with all those essential metal pieces mentioned throughout this book, and hundreds more; to John H. Blakey Ltd, of Radcliffe, Manchester, who makes ropes and *real* picture cord; and to my wife, Lys de Bray, author and artist, whose picture gallery, and its customers, revealed the need for this book.

A Note on Metric and Imperial Measurements

Throughout *Picture Framing and Hanging*, in line with its companion volumes in the series, measurements are given in metric, followed by the imperial equivalent.

But in this book it is by no means always the *exact* equivalent. When a dimension is given as, say, 'a clearance of 1mm', don't expect to see '0.03937in'! You will find instead '1/32 in', because what matters is that any measurement should be practical and familiar to the craftsman who is using it. If you are used to working in inches, continue to do so, because the imperial system was generated by engineers and craftsmen who wanted to work in simple, low numbers of feet, inches and pounds, not in hundreds of millimetres and grammes, which were more suited to the scientific world. Even the fractional inch, complicated as it looks to the metric-influenced, is more practical than the millimetre, because it is based on halving, which comes easily to the eye, so that sixteenths and thirty-seconds can be marked off using only a one-eighth rule. But just try estimating two millimetres with a centimetre rule!

The metric system is with us, however, and here to stay, and most of the materials and parts mentioned in this book are identified by their metric sizes because that is how they are now ordered and bought. But when it comes to pressures, '10,932 kilogrammes per square metre' is just too much. This book says '1 ton per square foot'.

Introduction

Pictures are made to be seen. But, too often, pictures that can bring gaiety to a room, that can mould into its decor, that can intrigue and interest and amuse, lie unseen. Photographs, prints from far-away places, sketches, posters, magazine cartoons, collages, dried flower arrangements – all lie in the dark, rolled up or flattened under the paraphernalia of the household.

As pieces of paper or material, that is where they will stay, enjoyed by no one, except on the few occasions when they might come to light in a clear-out, only to return again to their tombs. But, given rigidity, protection and an attractive mounting, they can become part of the home, and bring pleasure to the family and visitors for ever. And that is the purpose of picture framing.

There are many kinds of picture frame and many ways of mounting and hanging pictures. They range from the cheapest, simplest, moulded plastic, pre-sized frames to professionally produced custom-made mountings that might include a dozen different materials in the finished product. They can be ordered from a professional framer or they can be made at home. They can use different forms of assembly, different methods of protection, and countless combinations of woods, metals, board, paper, cloths and adhesives that can be selected to provide the most economical and optimum permanent protection for any type of picture.

This book is divided into three parts, each with a specific aim. Part One shows how the professional framer makes a finished product, the variations that he can offer, and how you can select the variations best suited to a particular picture. Part Two shows how to produce these frames and their variations in the home, taking account of the tooks available, which might range from a fully-equipped workshop to a Stanley knife and a rule. Finally, to help you enjoy your pictures to the full, Part Three suggests ways to group pictures, and shows how to hang them safely.

It is in Parts Two and Three that tricks of the trade are revealed and, to help spot them in the text, they are set in bold type and marked with the symbol →.

Part One

Types of Framing and Mounting

The 'Classic' Frame

The most common type of frame used for water colours, prints and many other types of pictures, is shown in Figure 1. It comprises many more components than is usually assumed, because many people believe that, in this apparently simple frame, the picture is held in place by being squeezed between the glass and the backing board, which is held to the frame with adhesive tape.

Anyone who has tried to make a frame at home in this way will know that, unless the picture itself is made of stiff card or board, it will start to buckle

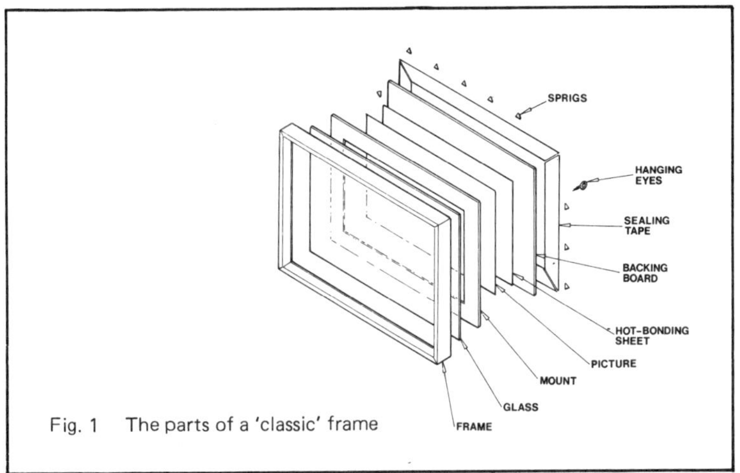

Fig. 1 The parts of a 'classic' frame

after a few days or even after a few hours. Temperature variations in the room give rise to different expansion and contraction rates in the various materials used, often worsened by trapped moisture, and buckling of the picture will usually appear near the edges and in bands across the centre. Once there, the buckles will never disappear.

The professional framer overcomes this problem by hot-bonding the picture to the backing board. The hot-bonding process uses a special double-sided adhesive sheet, a piece of which is cut to the size of the picture and laid under it. The picture, adhesive sheet and backing board are then placed in a powerful, heated press, which applies a pressure of about 1 ton per square foot at a temperature of about 100° C (212° F), for 20 to 30 seconds. When the press is opened, the picture is flat and rigid, and it will stay that way forever.

Despite the apparently disagreeable conditions inside the press, the hot-bonding process causes no harm to any type of picture, be it a photograph, drawing, water colour or print. Furthermore, the hot-bond sheet does not cause staining of the picture, which can arise with the use of wet adhesives.

The mount is cut to the same size as the picture, and its centre is then cut out, using a machine in which the cutting blade is angled at 45°, to provide what is called a 'mitred mount' (see Figure 2). The angled, mitred sides of the central aperture in a mitred mount present a more pleasing appearance than those of a 'straight-cut' mount, in which the cutting is done with a vertical blade.

The glass is cut to the size of the backing board and the parts are now ready for assembly into the frame.

The frame may be made from any of the hundreds of wood mouldings and metal sections that are widely

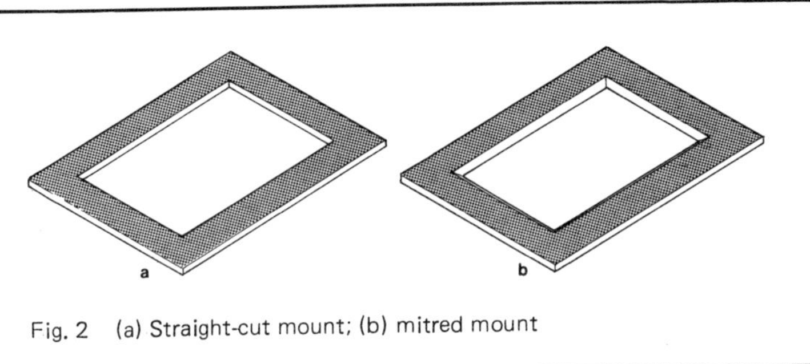

Fig. 2 (a) Straight-cut mount; (b) mitred mount

available. Typical wooden frames are made of straight-grained, seasoned hardwoods from Scandinavia, South and North America and Africa, routed to a wide variety of sections (see Figure 36, page 42) and finished in many colours and textures. To obtain the perfect 45° angle required at each corner of the frame, the professional framer employs a special machine in which the cutting is done by honed, high-tensile steel blades which chop through the moulding in one power-driven thrust, leaving a planed, smooth, angled corner. This machine will also deal with metal-finish frames, which have thin metal skins mounted on a hardwood core, but solid metal frames, made from rolled or extruded sections, are usually machine-sawn at the corners.

The four pieces of the frame, each cropped at 45° at each end, are then assembled together, with a smear of woodworking adhesive applied at each joint, and with fine steel pins driven in to lock them together while the adhesive sets.

The glass, which is carefully cleaned on its inside face before insertion, is then placed in the rebate of the frame, followed by the assembled mount, picture and backing board, and the whole lot is staked in place. Staking is accomplished by using a glazier's stapler which fires flat 'sprigs' (see Figure 46, page 62) into the inside edges of the frame while the picture assembly is pressed into the rebate, leaving a firm and rigid product. The gap between the backing board and the inside of the rear of the frame is then covered with adhesive tape to render the whole frame dust and dirt proof.

Two small pilot holes are then made in the back of the frame for later insertion of the hanging eyes and, finally, the corner pin heads and any small chips at the frame corners are touched up with coloured fillers, before the front of the glass, and the frame itself, are cleaned prior to wrapping and delivery.

Variations on the 'Classic' Frame

Mount Variations

Except in the case of water colours, mounts are a matter of personal choice, being selected for their appearance, for the way in which they can enhance a picture, or for purposes of decor.

For water colours they are essential, because no water colour should be allowed to rest directly behind the picture glass. Room-temperature variations, coupled with trapped moisture, can cause unavoidable condensation, in minute quantities, on the back of the glass, but these quantities can be enough to ruin a water colour. The thickness of the mount card itself is sufficient to protect the painting against this hazard.

For other types of picture, mounts need not be fitted at all, but in many cases their colour and texture, and sometimes their shape, do improve the appearance of a picture and can help it blend into the decor of a room. They are available in almost every conceivable colour and shade, from bright and strong to muted and subtle, and they can be supplied with soft finishes, such as silk, velvet and sprayed flock, which are particularly suitable for glassless frames.

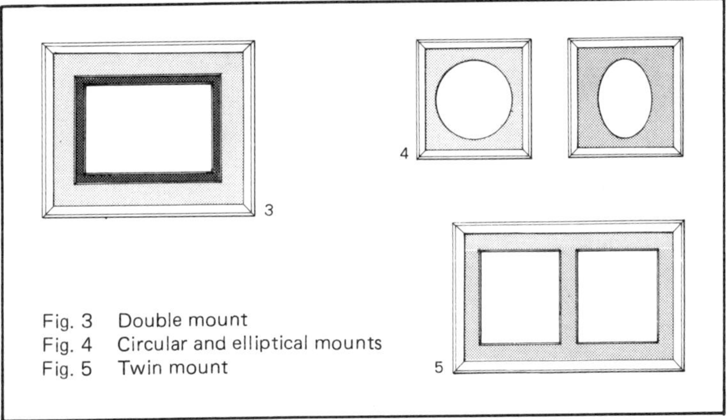

Fig. 3 Double mount
Fig. 4 Circular and elliptical mounts
Fig. 5 Twin mount

An attractive decorative touch is the use of double mounts (Figure 3). Here two mitred mounts are employed, in contrasting or blending colours, with the rear mount having a slightly smaller aperture than the main front mount. The result is a pleasing, inner frame of extra colour, achieved at very little extra cost.

Mounts can also be cut to circular or elliptical apertures, either mitred or unmitred, and these are particularly well-suited to portraits and some floral designs (see Figure 4).

For pairs of matched small pictures, twin mounting (see Figure 5) provides an attractive and economical solution. This can be extended to triplet and quadruplet mounting for three or more matching pictures, within the confines of the dimensions of standard mount card – usually about 75cm x 50cm (30in x 20in).

Reverse mounts can be used when the picture or material to be displayed cannot or must not be hot-bonded to a backing board. This would apply in the case of a picture with archival value, which might need to be removed later, intact and unaltered, or to a piece of fine lace or old parchment. In these cases

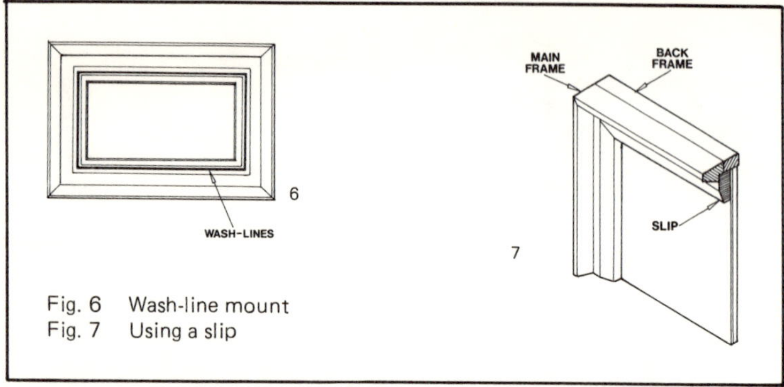

Fig. 6 Wash-line mount
Fig. 7 Using a slip

the picture or the material is simply laid on to coloured mount card and is trapped in place behind the glass. While material such as lace will lie satisfactorily flat in this arrangement, buckling of paper cannot be avoided.

Mounts can themselves be decorated in a manner known as 'wash-line' (see Figure 6), in which the mount, after cutting, has fine single or double lines drawn on it around the aperture. The lines may be black or coloured, and often the space between double lines is filled in with a light colour wash.

Slips

The use of slips is shown in Figure 7. Slips are, in effect, 'add-on' framing sections to augment the shape and appearance of the main frame. They are usually simpler in shape than main frames, often tapered, and sometimes have a very light additional moulding, in another colour, on their inside edges. They can be in plain wood, or can carry different finishes in paint and in materials such as hessian and velvet. Most professional framers carry stocks of such materials, in ranges of colours, that can be cut and stuck to any of the slips that are available, providing a totally custom-made frame for a special picture.

As Figure 7 shows, the extra thickness of a slip

may call for an additional back frame, which is coloured and finished to match the main frame, but mouldings with extra-deep rebates, often used for oil paintings, may be used instead (see Figure 36, page 42).

Double Framing

Another form of custom-made framing that can enhance the appearance of a picture is double framing (see Figure 8). Here the picture, which may be mounted or unmounted, is placed in a relatively simple frame, which is then fixed to a larger, heavier board, usually with screws from the rear. This board is in turn mounted in a heavier, more complex frame, and the gap between the two frames can than be filled with any colour, or any material, such as hessian or carpet or even wallpaper, to suit both the picture and the decor of the room.

An alternative form of double framing, sometimes known as reversed or embossed double framing, is shown in Figure 9. Here, the weights of the two frames are reversed, the inner one being the heavier of the two. Again, the gap between the frames can be filled with any colour or material.

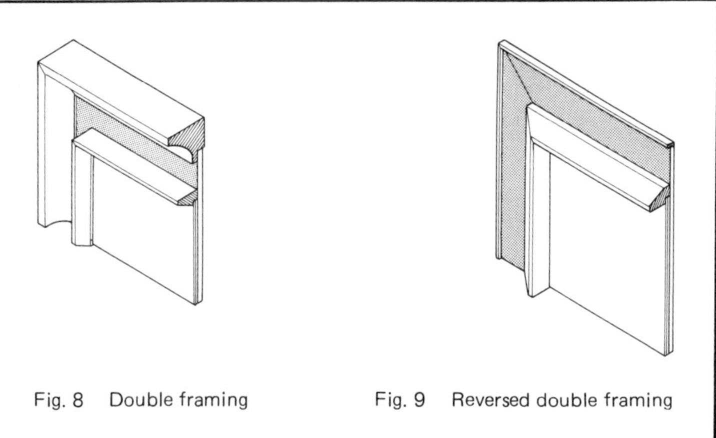

Fig. 8 Double framing

Fig. 9 Reversed double framing

Box Framing

To mount three-dimensional pictures, such as collages, dried flowers or plaster mouldings, it is necessary to use a box frame (see Figure 10) in which the front glass is mounted at a suitable distance from the backing board. As with slips, this requires the use of an additional rear frame, finished to match the main frame.

Box frames can be doubled and used as display cases for items such as coins. In such cases, the coins, mounted in punched-out holes on a central panel, are placed between two framed glasses that show the obverse and reverse sides of the coins.

Non-Rectangular Frames

Although the vast majority of frames are rectangular, it is possible to obtain non-rectangular frames to suit special pictures. An example of a non-rectangular frame, of hexagonal shape, is shown in Figure 11. Most power cropping machines can be set to accept the different corner angles required for six- or eight-sided shapes, but other polygons with odd numbers of sides need to be cut by hand, which always involves extra cost.

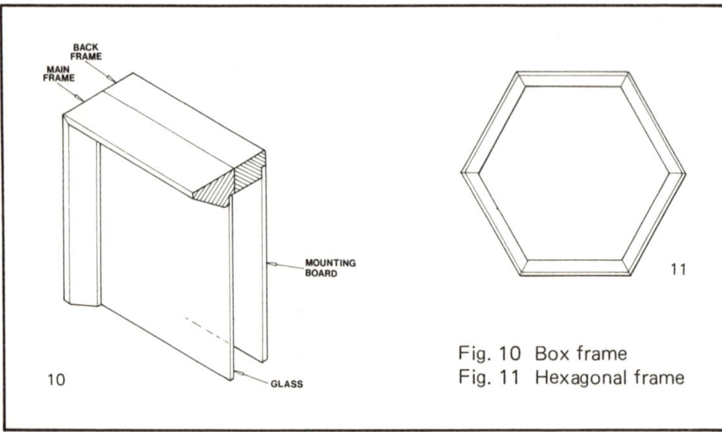

Fig. 10 Box frame
Fig. 11 Hexagonal frame

Circular frames can also be obtained, but usually in standard diameters and with a more restricted range of mouldings. Special circular frames can be made to order, as can elliptical frames made from parts of circles, but these need to be specially turned on a lathe and this can be expensive.

Non-Reflecting Glass

If a picture is to be hung opposite a large window or below a bright light, non-reflecting glass (NRG) should be used instead of plain glass. Both sides of NRG are very finely stippled, so that light falling on it is diffused, unlike plain glass which reflects light like a mirror, giving disturbing reflections that can spoil the view of a picture.

Despite the surface stippling, the transparency of NRG is unaffected when it is placed on a picture. If it touches the picture (that is, with no mount in the frame) it becomes practically invisible because of its non-reflecting properties, giving the impression that the picture has been protected by a very hard varnish. Even when mounted off the picture by the thickness of a mount card, the loss of transparency is imperceptible, but if the gap behind the glass reaches 3mm (1/8 in) or so, the definition of the picture begins to deteriorate.

Glassless Frames

In very large frames, the weight of the glass becomes the major component of the overall weight of the picture and can lead to problems in frame joints and in hanging the picture safely. In such cases it is possible to dispense with the glass and to protect the picture by heat-sealing it. This is a similar process to hot-bonding (page 12) but in this case a heated press is used to fuse a sheet of transparent film to the face of the picture, which needs to be suitably stiffened before sealing. As with hot-bonding, the heat and pressure have no adverse effect on the picture, and the protecting film is washable. This type of film is used in block mounting (page 22) and may, of course, be used on small pictures as well.

Standing Frames

Any 'classic' frame, and most of the variations mentioned in the preceding pages, can be converted to standing frames by fixing suitable struts to the backing board (see Figure 12). The struts, which are usually made of plywood or hardboard, are fixed to the backing board with a strut hinge which allows the strut to lie flat for transport or packing.

Simpler Frames

Oil Paintings

Usually the most expensive pictures to buy, oil paintings need only the simplest of frames, as they are already self-protected by their own hardness and by varnish, and should remain uncovered so that brush-work details can be appreciated. The canvas, stretched on its own wooden frame, is simply clipped or screwed into a suitable frame with an extra-deep rebate (see Figure 36, page 42).

Exhibition and Display Frames

For temporary display purposes, such as at exhibitions, pictures can be adequately protected by being trapped behind a sheet of glass, which is clipped to a matching-sized sheet of blockboard, chipboard or plywood, as shown in Figure 13. For lighter display purposes – that is, where the picture is not going to be subjected to the rough-and-tumble of erection and dismantling at exhibitions – the backing board may be reduced to a sheet of hardboard, with the

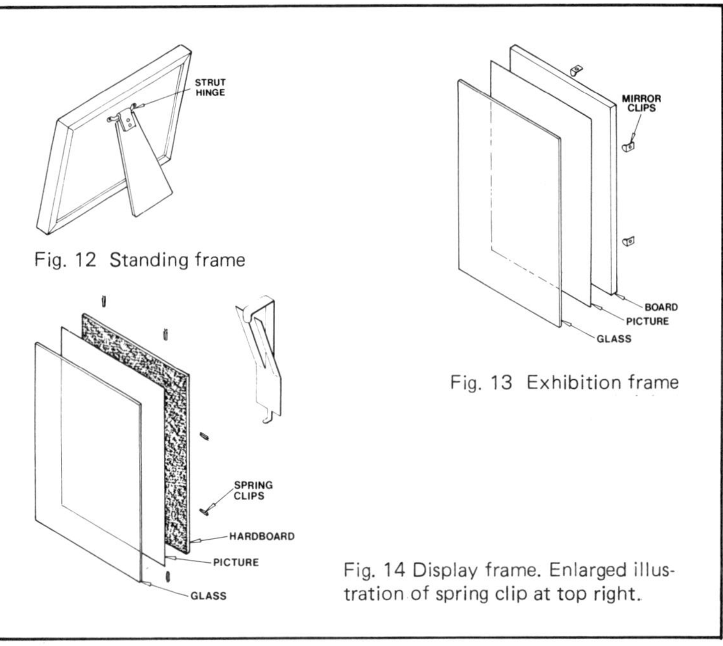

Fig. 12 Standing frame

Fig. 13 Exhibition frame

Fig. 14 Display frame. Enlarged illustration of spring clip at top right.

The small peg at the bottom of each clip, shown in detail in Figure 14, is used to lock the clip in position. Hardboard backs can be supplied with shallow-sawn slots to accept these pegs, but small holes, drilled through the hardboard at the correct distance in from the edge, are equally good.

As the edges of the glass are unprotected, they must be ground and chamfered before assembly. assembly held together by spring clips, sometimes known as Emo clips, as shown in Figure 14. These clips provide a neat, unobtrusive mounting and are quite suitable for use in the home, but the picture itself must be stiffened to prevent buckling if it is to be displayed in this way for any length of time.

Plastic and Ready-Made Frames

A large variety of ready-made or ready-to-assemble

frames in woods and plastics can be found in do-it-yourself shops, artists' suppliers and hardware stores. Some sell frames moulded in one piece, supplied with ready-cut glass and backing boards, while others provide cut, mitred lengths of framing mouldings that can be clipped together, with or without glass and board. Many of them present a very pleasing appearance when assembled, but all carry the risk of picture buckling if the picture itself is not made of thick card or has not been bonded down. Even a heavy-weight photographic enlargement is not stiff enough to stop buckling if it is simply trapped between the glass and the backing board in such frames, and bonding down must be carried out. Methods of bonding down in the home are explained in Part Two (page 58).

Block Mounting

One of the cheapest ways of protecting and presenting a picture attractively is to use block mounting. Here, as seen in Figure 15, a sandwich of heat-sealing film, the picture and hot-bonding film is placed on a sheet of chipboard and the whole is subjected to heat and pressure in a heated press. The edges of the chipboard are usually chamfered to the size of the picture and painted matt black, although other colours can be specified. The front film, which provides permanent protection for the picture, is washable.

Metal Frames

Attractive frames can be made relatively cheaply by using one of the several metal framing sections that are available. The sections (see Figure 16) are made of rolled or extruded aluminium, usually with a bright, chemically applied finish that gives a silver or golden colour to the frame. As can be seen from the drawing, the framing sections are machine-mitred to length and then slipped on to the glass/picture/backing

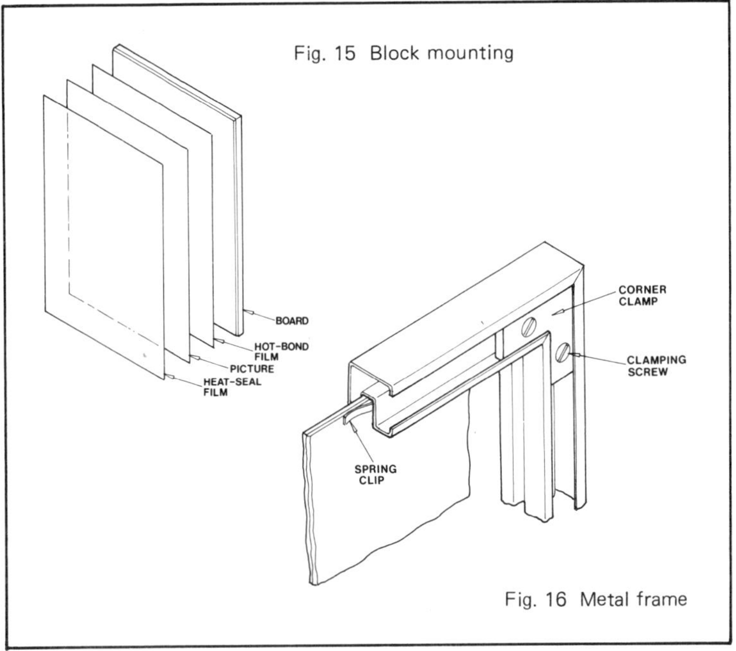

Fig. 15 Block mounting

Fig. 16 Metal frame

board sandwich, which is retained in place by internal spring clips. The corners of the frame are held together by metal corner clamps which are pulled tightly into the inside of the rear flanges of the frame by clamping screws which push against an internal face.

Passe-Partout

There does not appear to be any professional framer left in Britain who will offer passe-partout, because of the amount of hand-work involved and because passe-partout tape is unobtainable.

The tape for passe-partout (meaning, literally, to 'pass all' or to 'fit all') was specially marked and scored to make the job of fitting, folding and cutting the tape relatively simple. Without it, the making of a passe-partout frame becomes a job requiring time, patience and a steady hand, but the final product is

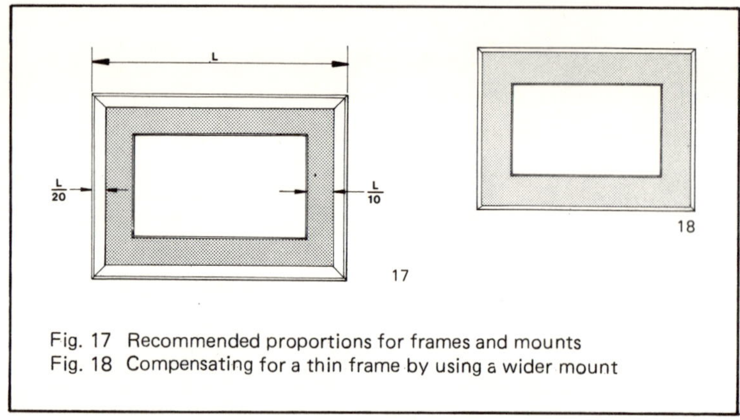

Fig. 17 Recommended proportions for frames and mounts
Fig. 18 Compensating for a thin frame by using a wider mount

attractive and cheap, and the way of accomplishing the task at home is shown in Part Two (page 68).

Choosing Frames and Mounts

Frame and Mount Sizes

The appearance of a picture can be spoilt if the sizes of the chosen frame and mount are out of proportion with the picture. A general guide to frame and mount sizes is given in Figure 17, which shows that the width of the frame moulding, when viewed from the front, should be about one-twentieth of the longest dimension of the overall picture. If a mount is to be fitted, its nominal width should be not less than twice that of the moulding, that is about one-tenth of the longest dimension. As an example, if the complete picture is to be 50cm (20in) long, the moulding should be 2.5cm (1in) wide, and the mount 5cm (2in) wide.

This proportioning of moulding size is not only a matter of aesthetics. It concerns structural strength and safety too, because the width of the moulding determines its capacity to carry the weight of the picture glass and controls the size of the hanging eyes that can be screwed into it. The safe loads that can be carried by hanging eyes, and thus by moulding sizes, are shown in Part Two (page 66).

Sometimes, for the sake of economy, or because an old frame is already available, a thinner moulding has to be used. In such cases, with adequate safety precautions for hanging, as explained in Part Two, the mount should be widened to compensate for the thinness of the frame (see Figure 18) so that the overall width of the moulding plus the mount is maintained. For the same example, if the moulding is only 1cm (½in) wide, the mount width should be increased to 6.5cm (2½in).

Mount Proportions: The 'Golden Ratio'

Modern practice calls for cutting mount apertures at a constant width from the edge of the mount (pictures A and C in Figure 19) because it is easier and quicker, and therefore more economical, to set the mount-cutting machine for constant-width cutting.

But many older pictures, and some modern ones too, use a deeper base for the mount, particularly for vertical pictures (B in Figure 19), and sometimes for horizontal pictures (D in Figure 19) where the

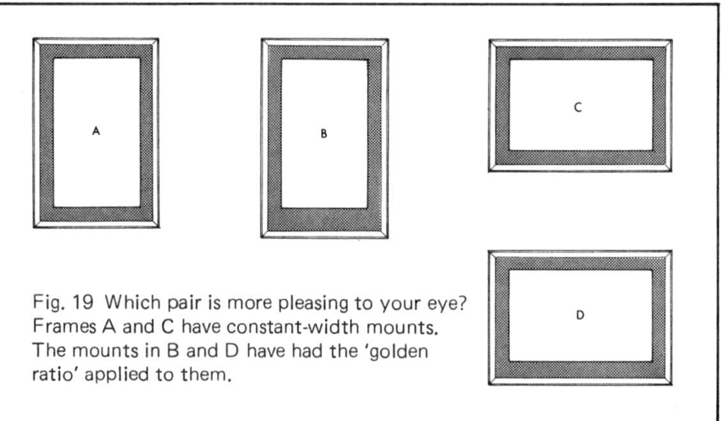

Fig. 19 Which pair is more pleasing to your eye? Frames A and C have constant-width mounts. The mounts in B and D have had the 'golden ratio' applied to them.

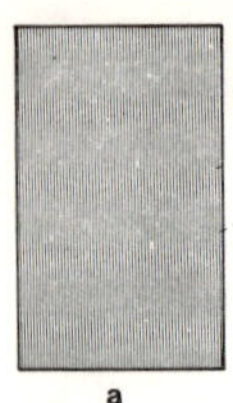

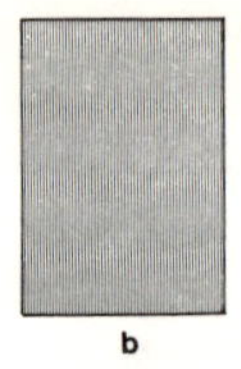

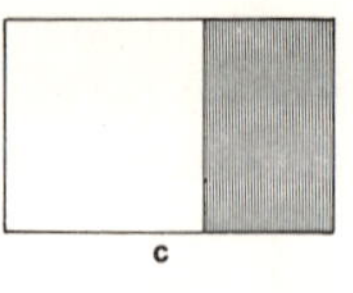

Fig. 20 (a) The 'golden rectangle'. Height-to-width ratio – 1.62:1
(b) International A-size paper. Height-to-width ratio – 1.41:1
(c) Cutting a square off a 'golden rectangle' leaves another 'golden rectangle'

increase in width at the base is subtle but perceptible. The use of such extra depth is a matter of personal taste – some people prefer the modern constant width – but without it the constant-width mounted picture appears to be 'sunk' in its frame.

The amount of extra depth of the base is not guesswork – it is founded on what is called the 'golden ratio', familiar to the ancient Greeks, who used it in architecture and sculpture, and to medieval and Renaissance mathematicians. The ratio, sometimes called 'Greek squares' or the 'Fibonacci series', is related to a series of numbers in which each number is the sum of the preceding two, i.e. 1, 2, 3, 5, 8, 13, 21, 34, etc. If such numbers are applied to the height and width of a piece of paper (or a doorway or a window) the resulting rectangle is said to be particularly attractive to the eye. The higher the numbers, the more closely they approach the golden ratio of 1.62:1 (Figure 20a). The defunct foolscap writing paper (13in x 8in) was very close to this ratio, and Figure 20b shows, for comparison, the height-width ratio of modern international A-size paper (1.41:1) on which many drawings and paintings are made. One of the peculiar properties of the golden rectangle is that cutting a square off it (Figure

20c) leaves another golden rectangle, and cutting a square off that leaves another, and so on.

The professional framer who is aware of this ratio applies it to mount cutting in a variety of ways. For horizontal pictures he adopts a compromise between two measurements – the diagonal of a horizontal golden ratio and that of a vertical. This is shown in Figure 21. Point 0 is the bottom left-hand corner of the mount aperture, and line 0A is the diagonal of a horizontal golden rectangle, lying at 32° below horizontal. Line 0B is the diagonal of a vertical golden rectangle, at 58° below, and point C is exactly half-way between A and B. It is point C that marks where the bottom of the mount is to be cut, and it lies at 48° below the horizontal. This angle, which replaces the normal 45° used at the top corners of the mount, results in a base that is just about 10 per cent wider than the sides and top of the mount, and for practical purposes the framer uses simply that 10 per cent. Thus, for a mount that is 50mm (2in)

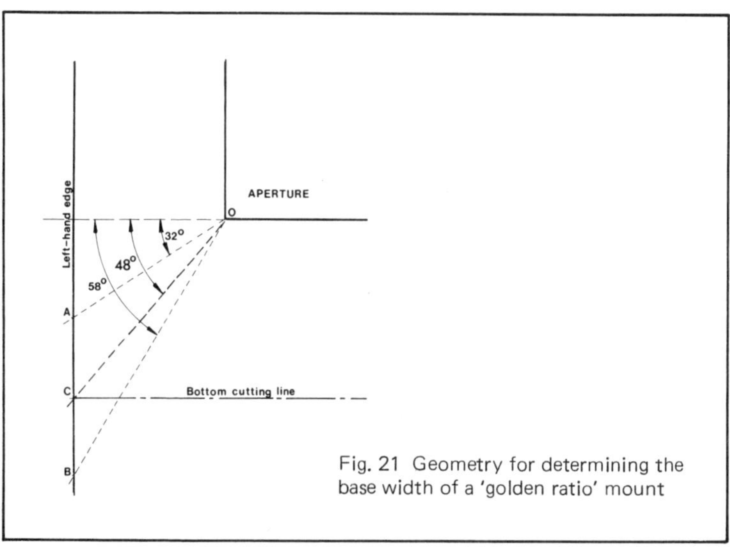

Fig. 21 Geometry for determining the base width of a 'golden ratio' mount

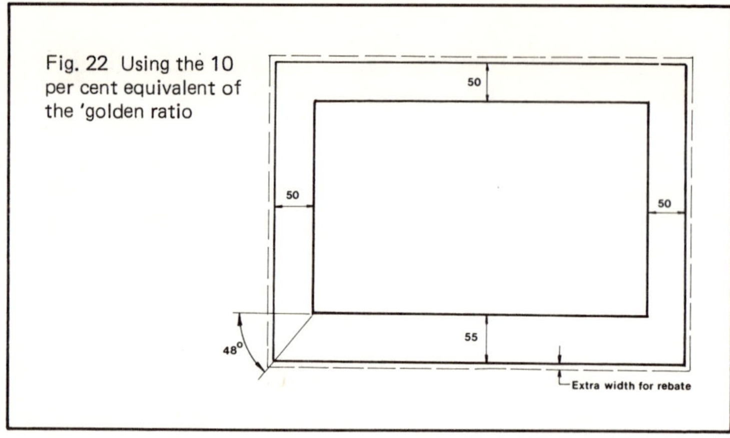

Fig. 22 Using the 10 per cent equivalent of the 'golden ratio

wide at its top and sides, the base is cut to 55mm (2.2in) – see Figure 22.

These are the dimensions that are supposed to show when the mount is fitted inside the rebate of the frame, and to allow for this the perfectionist adds the rebate width to the final dimensions of the mount, as shown in Figure 22.

For vertical pictures, two alternative applications of the golden ratio are adopted. For pictures with height/width ratios up to that of the golden ratio (about 1.6 to 1) the bottom of the mount is cut simply where an extension of the picture diagonal cuts the side of the mount (see Figure 23), and this becomes a normal 45° position for a square picture. For tall, skinny pictures, this results in a base that is too deep, and the framer reverts to the 48° (10 per cent extra) base depth (see Figure 24).

The golden ratio can be applied to the dimensions of a mount aperture to compensate for the proportions of a picture that looks too long or too fat, as shown in Figure 25, but this practice too is a matter of personal taste.

In some cases, an extra-deep base may be called

for to accommodate an additional cut-out in which a picture title can be placed (see Figure 26).

Colours and Textures

Choosing the colour and texture of a frame and mount to suit a particular picture can be made a little easier by following some general guide lines that will help to ensure the most attractive presentation.

The colours of the frame and the mount should either contrast or blend with each other, the colour

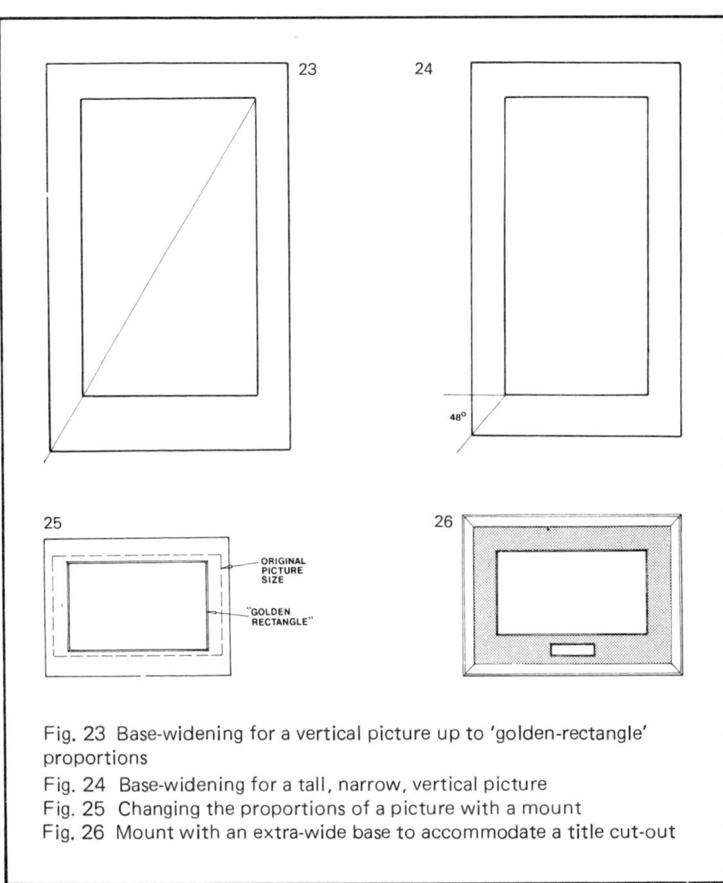

Fig. 23 Base-widening for a vertical picture up to 'golden-rectangle' proportions
Fig. 24 Base-widening for a tall, narrow, vertical picture
Fig. 25 Changing the proportions of a picture with a mount
Fig. 26 Mount with an extra-wide base to accommodate a title cut-out

of the wall on which the picture is to be hung, and the general tone of the picture itself. Here 'tone' refers not only to the tints in the picture but to its content as well. A gentle, countryside scene would be shattered by a bright red mount, but would sit happily in a grey-green, while another type of green picture, such as an impressionist painting with bars of green across it, would overwhelm a subtly-coloured mount but sit well inside one of strong yellow or black.

The frame acts as a transfer colour between the mount and the wall, blending in with both but with sufficient contrast to delineate it clearly. If the wall is white, a white frame would be lost against it, but at the same time a dark-coloured frame must not clash with the chosen colour of the mount. This is where multi-coloured frames, with fine stripes of colour or gold on a background colour, or with inserts of hessian, become useful. So does double framing, in which the gap between the two frames can be used as a transfer colour.

Here are just a few examples of the countless colour choices that can be made:

WALL COLOUR	PICTURE TONE	MOUNT COLOUR	FRAME COLOUR
white	blue – soft	medium blue	dark blue stripe
white	white/red – harsh	red/orange	aluminium/black
pale blue	blue – soft	dark blue	white/gold
pale blue	white/red – harsh	dark grey	black/gold
dark brown	blue – soft	grey-blue	striped oak
dark brown	white/red – harsh	dark brown	white

With the sizes of frames and mounts based on the recommendations given in the preceding pages, and the colours chosen, further choice can be made in textures. Mount card can be supplied with soft finishes, such as silk, linen and flock, and these finishes can help to soften the overall appearance of a picture. Frame finishes can range from the smooth, gloss black of the simple 'certificate' moulding (used widely for framing certificates) to the heavy rococo scrolls in cast plaster used for the traditional framing of oil paintings. In between there are mouldings made of simple stained and varnished woods and with gloss and matt painted finishes. These finishes and textures should be considered in relation to the decor of the room – to its modernity, its antiquity, its coolness or its warmth.

When having a picture framed professionally, it is a good idea to take along a piece of the wallpaper or a piece of card with the wall colour painted on it, so that the whole combination of picture, mount, frame and wall can be examined and the best choice made from the samples available at the framer.

Part Two

Picture Framing in the Home

Frames

Mouldings

The most complex job in picture framing at home is the manufacture of the frame itself, and before embarking on the job, which is described in detail on the following pages, the availability of tools in the home workshop has to be considered, because what is available determines the type of frame moulding that should be chosen.

If you are the fortunate owner of a fully equipped woodworking shop, with a bench saw or bandsaw with tilting tables, a bench sander and planer and a drill press, you can choose practically any moulding you like from which to make the frame, because you should be able to achieve the perfect 45° mitres required at each frame corner. **Without that perfection, badly-made mitres can never be corrected on finished mouldings (that is, mouldings that are already coloured when purchased) without damaging the finish or showing ugly fillings in the frame corners.** ←

If this sort of machinery is not available, you have two alternatives:

1. Find a professional picture framer who will supply you with your chosen moulding cropped to length. His machine cropper will make the perfect mitres required, and your job is eased enormously, but be prepared for refusal or for a very high price for

the work, because the framer has to cover the depreciation costs of his specialist equipment and he does this normally in his pricing for a complete picture-framing job. Without the whole job to recover his costs, he has to charge a lot extra in compensation.

2. Buy unfinished, raw-timber moulding, which can be subsequently filled with plastic wood if errors appear, and then be coloured and finished after frame assembly.

In either case, with finished or unfinished mouldings, make your choice of moulding based on the recommendations given in Part 1, and check, too, that the rebate depth is adequate for your glass, → picture and backing board (see Figure 45). **Make sure, also, that you can cut all four frame members out of one piece of moulding, even if this means buying a piece several metres long. While two shorter pieces might appear to be identical, the chances are that they will differ by a fraction of a millimetre, and with this difference, the mitres will never match.** Finally, check the entire length of the moulding for damage or blemishes. If any are apparent, reject it.

Measuring

The method of determining the overall length and width of a frame for a given picture is shown in Figure 27, and the procedure is as follows:

1. Measure the moulding depth D. Note that this does *not* include the depth of the moulding rebate.

2. Measure the length of the glass GL. Note that it is best to cut the glass *before* making the frame (see the section on glass cutting, page 54) because it is easier to adjust the frame size to a piece of glass than to alter the glass size to suit the frame.

3. Decide frame-to-glass clearance C. For pictures up to 50cm (20in) length, this should be taken as 1mm ($^1/_{32}$ in). For larger pictures, take 2mm ($^1/_{16}$ in).

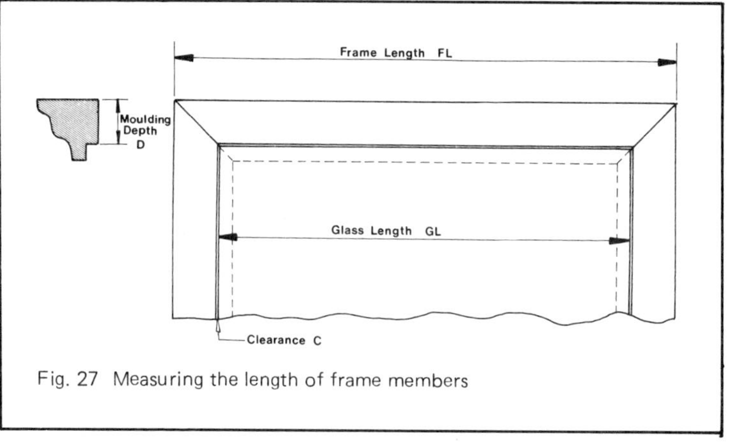

Fig. 27 Measuring the length of frame members

Then the overall length of the moulding to be cut is:

FL = GL + 2D + 2C

or, in non-mathematical terms:

Frame length = Glass length plus twice moulding depth plus twice the clearance.

The same formula applies, of course, to the height of the picture, based on glass height.

Remember to work wholly in millimetres or in inches. For example, if the glass is 500mm long and the moulding depth is 20mm, then the frame length is:

500 + (2 x 20) + (2 x 1) = 542mm.

Marking Off

The moulding now needs to be marked off to the dimensions calculated above. Two tools should be used for this process. The first, shown in Figure 28, is a 90° carpenter's try-square, and with it two lines are drawn across the outside of the moulding, spaced at the correct distance apart to give the calculated frame length. **For accuracy, use a hard-grade carpen-** ⟵

ter's pencil to draw the lines: a properly sharpened carpenter's pencil (sanded flat to a chisel point) will draw the line right up against the edge of the square without blunting, which a round pencil cannot do.

The second tool required for marking-off is a 45° try-square (shown in Figure 29) with which 45° lines are drawn across the back of the moulding, starting from where the 90° lines touch the back face. These 45° lines should be drawn clearly and sharply because it is they that will be used later when bringing the moulding exactly to length.

Make sure that the 45° lines are pointing the right way! It is all too easy to draw them and then cut the mitres, only to find that the mitres are reversed and suited only to an inside-out frame. Remember that the *outside* edge of the frame is the longest dimension, and that the 45° lines must point *inwards* from the ends of the frame.

Cutting

Depending on what tools are available, cutting of the moulding to length can be accomplished by machine or by hand. In either case, the exact point of cutting is determined by what *finishing* machinery or tools are available.

If the home workshop does not have a bench sander or planer or a planing jig (see page 40), the moulding has to be cut to length exactly on the 45° lines drawn on the back of the moulding, and no further finishing can be applied to the mitred ends. → **Any attempt to sand them or plane them to length by hand, without the assistance of machine tables or special jigs, will wreck the accuracy of the mitres, which will expose open joints, at the front of the frame and round its edges, when they are assembled.**

In this situation it is best to use unfinished, raw-timber moulding, so that, after assembly, any open

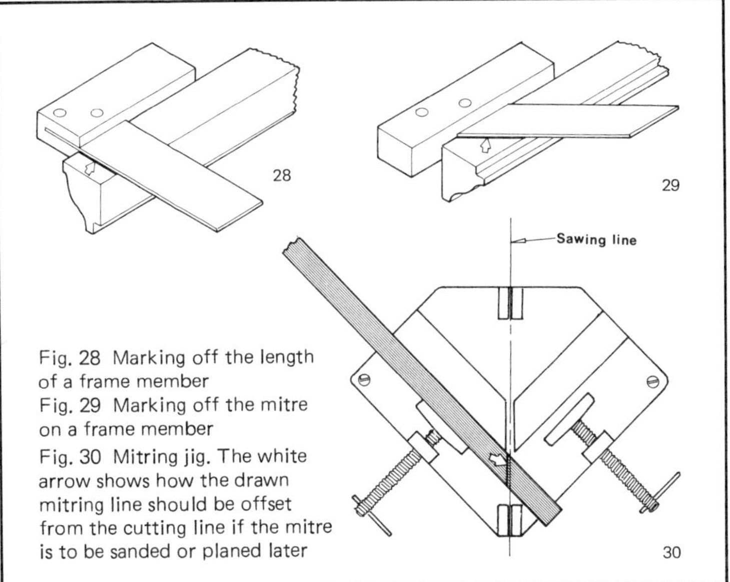

Fig. 28 Marking off the length of a frame member

Fig. 29 Marking off the mitre on a frame member

Fig. 30 Mitring jig. The white arrow shows how the drawn mitring line should be offset from the cutting line if the mitre is to be sanded or planed later

joints can be filled with plastic wood prior to finishing. (See the section on frame finishing, page 45).

Without a bench sander or planer, it is unlikely that the workshop contains a tilting table bandsaw, which can make a near-perfect sawn mitre, and the moulding must be hand-sawn to length using a mitring jig (see Figure 30). Many makes of mitring jig are available in do-it-yourself shops, and the best of them have adjustable saw guides, which can be set to fit the blade thickness of the saw to be used. A fine-tooth (thirty-two teeth to the inch) tenon saw is the best tool for the job, reserved exclusively for cutting mouldings. It should never be allowed out of the workshop for sawing off old branches in the garden! The height of the blade (from the teeth to the blade stiffener) must be sufficient to ensure that the stiffener does not foul the tops of the blade guides, which should be set so that the blade just slides freely within them.

The moulding is placed into the mitring jig, as shown in Figure 30, with the clamping vice run up lightly against it so that it can be slid into the correct position for cutting. In Figure 30 the white arrow shows how the 45° drawn line should be offset from the cutting line to allow for machine finishing later, but in the absence of finishing machines or jigs, the line has to be brought exactly to the edge of the saw. It is easiest, of course, to have this line visible when lining up, with the moulding clamped backface-up in the jig, and this is quite acceptable if the mitre is to be machine- or jig-finished later. But if it cannot be, and if the sawing has to take place exactly on the line, then the moulding must be placed backface-down in the jig so that the saw cuts cleanly into the front of the moulding and leaves a furry edge at the back, which can be sanded off later. In this case, with the 45° line no longer visible, the moulding must be positioned so that the first 90° measurement line, drawn on its outer edge, falls just below the edge of the saw.

With the moulding correctly positioned below the saw, which can be slipped into its guides while positioning, the clamping vice is then tightened up, ensuring that the moulding is lying flat against the jig base and snugly against its wall. Then, using very little pressure – hardly more than the weight of the saw itself – gently saw through the moulding and remove it from the jig for the next cut.

→ **With machinery or jigs available for finishing mitres, the cutting line should be offset by about 1mm (1/32 in), as shown in Figure 30, and the moulding can be cut from the front or the back, the back being easier because the 45° cutting line is in view.**

With bench or bandsaws, with or without tilting tables, a rough cut can be made, again offset from the

45° marked line for subsequent finishing of the mitre, which can be accomplished by sanding or planing.

Mitre Sanding

A rotary sanding machine, with a tilting table, will provide the perfect 45° mitre corner after rough cutting. **Before using it on a picture moulding, however, check the accuracy of the 45° table-tilt marker by sanding up two pieces of scrap hardwood or moulding and placing them together inside a 90° try-square. More often than not, it will be found that the so-called 45° is not that at all, and the mitre will exhibit a yawning gap at one extremity. Correct the table marker accordingly.**

If a tilting table is not fitted to the machine, a 45° sanding jig needs to be made (see Figure 31). This can be made from any scrap pieces of softwood (although hardwood is better) and its own accuracy, after manufacture, can be checked as explained in the paragraph above. It is, of course, essential that the front edge of the sanding table, on which the jig slides, must be exactly parallel to the face of the rotary sander. If the sander is not a self-contained machine, that is, if it has to be set up each time as an accessory to a power drill, then its accuracy must be checked each time it is set up.

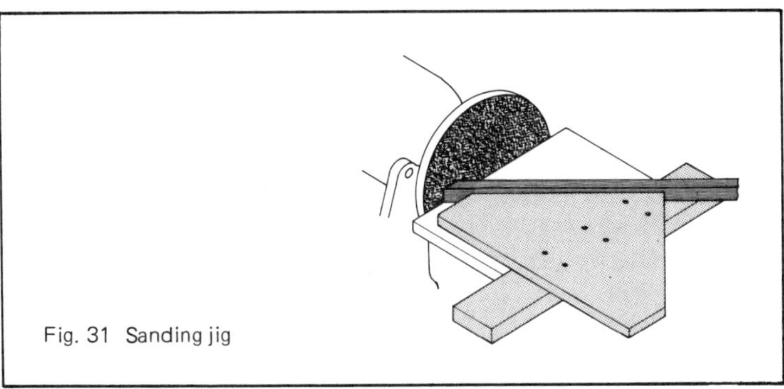

Fig. 31 Sanding jig

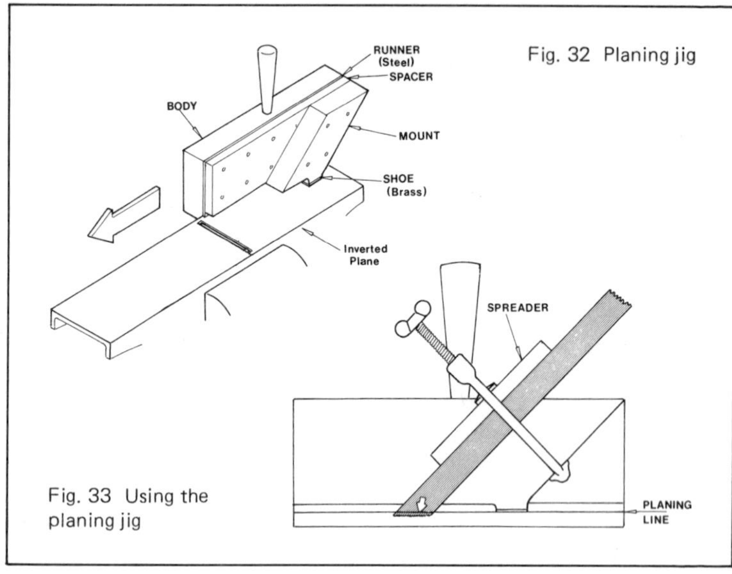

Fig. 32 Planing jig

Fig. 33 Using the planing jig

Mitre Planing

There are still framing craftsmen around who can hand-plane a mitre to a perfect 45° using no more than a small hand plane and a woodworker's vice. This is beyond the capability of most of the rest of humanity, even skilled cabinet makers who, in the days of hand-made furniture, made or bought planing jigs of the type shown in Figure 32. The accomplished do-it-yourselfer can construct his own, sized to suit his largest plane, using it as shown in Figure 33. These two drawings show how, when a rough-cut moulding is clamped to the jig with a G-cramp, using a wood load spreader to protect the moulding and to hold it rigidly against the mount, the moulding is passed forwards repeatedly over the plane blade, which is set to minimum cut. At each pass, a light planing cut is taken off the moulding, initially at a slight angle until, when the brass shoe touches the base of the plane, the mitre is finished at

45°, exactly square, with a smooth finish equivalent to that provided by the professional machine cropper.

Note that, in making such a jig, the steel runner plate must be thin enough to clear the plane blade as it slides by, and that the bottom of the brass shoe must be exactly level with the bottom of the runner. All other dimensions can be selected to suit the user. And, as in all woodworking practice, note too that the plane blade must be *sharp.*

Frame Jointing

The joints of a wood-moulding frame are held together by adhesive, not by pins. The pins are driven in simply to hold the mitred corners together while the adhesive sets. Indeed, if a belt corner cramp is available (see Figure 34) and sufficient care is taken to ensure that the whole assembly is dead square before it is laid aside to set, there is no need for pins at all. The professional framer invariably uses pins, however, for two reasons. First, he has several dozen, or even hundreds of frames passing through his workshop at times, and it would be uneconomic to have to provide a belt cramp for each one. Secondly, it is quicker to pin a frame together than to set it up and square it in a cramp. The framing craftsman can glue and pin the four corners of a frame perfectly square in less than half a minute.

The jointing operation is called 'pinning' because it

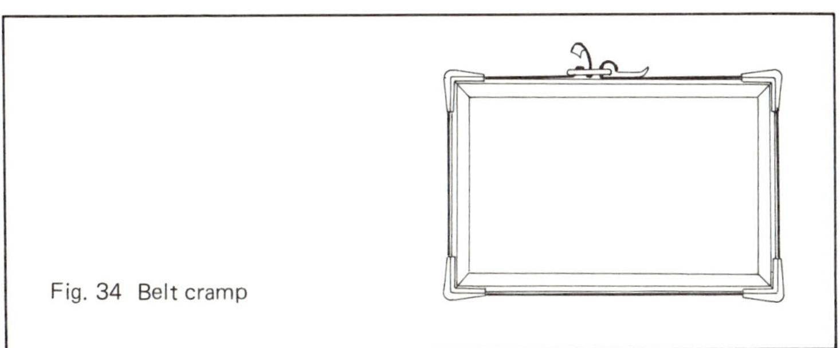

Fig. 34 Belt cramp

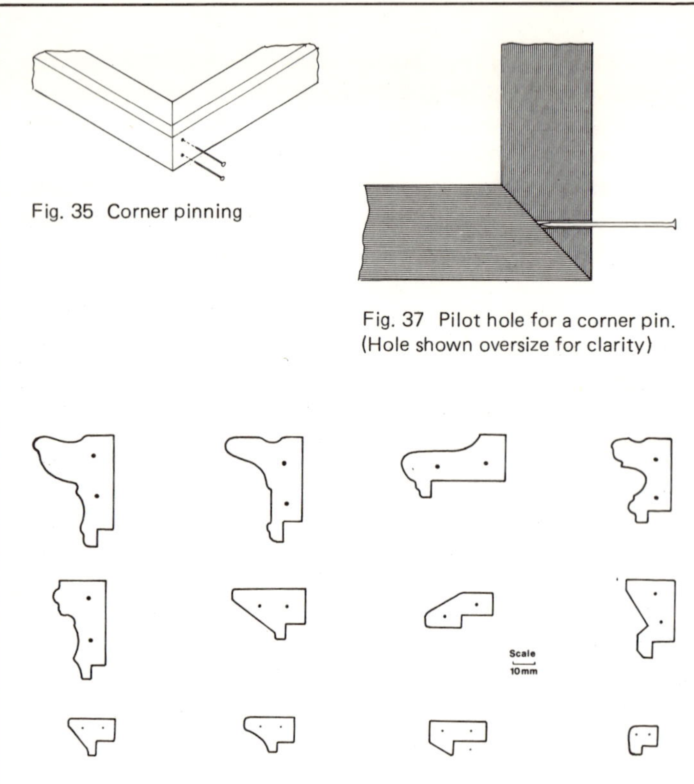

Fig. 35 Corner pinning

Fig. 37 Pilot hole for a corner pin. (Hole shown oversize for clarity)

Fig. 36 Typical moulding sections, showing recommended positions and sizes of moulding pins. Note the extra-deep rebates in the third row from the left to accommodate slips (Figure 7) without using an extra back frame, or oil-painting canvases

uses *moulding pins*, not panel pins or nails. Only moulding pins are fine enough to drive into hardwood mouldings so near to the cut end of the wood without splitting it, and even then their position has to be carefully controlled.

Figure 35 shows the nominal positions of the two pins that are driven into each corner, while Figure 36 shows more clearly the optimum positions and sizes of pins for typical mouldings. Note that, as the moulding sections get larger, they call for bigger pins, and the bigger the pin the more liable it is to split the timber unless a pilot hole is drilled first (see Figure 37). The pilot hole (shown oversize for clarity in the drawing) should be a fraction under the size of the pin, and the correct drill for the hole should be selected as follows. Place the pin in the jaws of a sliding caliper and close the jaws tightly on the pin. Lock the jaws and remove the pin. Now select a drill that just slides loosely into the jaws. With metric drills this means having available drills in ½-mm steps, and with imperial drills in 1/64-in steps.

If the mitres have been finished to an exact and smooth 45°, square to the moulding, there is no need to use an assembly jig because they will pull the frame square and flat as they are joined. The assembly procedure is as follows.

Clamp the first piece of moulding, face up, to the front edge of the worktable, using one or two G-clamps and a piece of soft timber to protect the moulding face. Brush a smear of PVA woodworking adhesive on to the right-hand mitred end (if you are right-handed) and bring the next piece of moulding in contact with it. Place the first pin in position, as shown in Figure 35 and in accordance with the recommendations given in Figure 36, and lightly tap it into the moulding until it is rigid but has not yet broken through.

Now position the second piece of moulding so that it is offset from the clamped piece, as shown in Figure 38. This is to overcome the subsequent slip that will occur when you are driving the pin home, and the amount of initial offset to apply becomes a matter of habit after some practice. Now, guiding the position of the left piece with your left hand, drive the pin in farther, ensuring that, as it bites into the

Fig. 38 Overcoming slip during pinning by off-setting during pin driving

clamped piece, the two mouldings are absolutely flush at the front and that the two mitres are exactly matched, with no slip. If you are satisfied, drive the pin fully home, and put in the second pin.

If you are not satisfied, pull out the half-driven pin with a pair of pliers, taking care not to damage the moulding, and try again.

At this stage, deal with excess glue in the joint. If the right amount of adhesive has been applied and the joint is good and tight after pinning, a slight 'weep' of adhesive should appear between the two mitres all round the joint. If you are using finished (coloured or varnished) moulding, wipe it off now with a piece of rag. **If you are using unfinished, raw-timber moulding, leave it to dry a little and then cut it away with a sharp craft knife. If you don't leave it but attempt to wipe it away while it is wet, it will smear into the grain and prevent the wood from accepting stain or other finishes to be applied later and a patchy finish will result.**

Repeat the process for the second joint, this time with the second piece of moulding clamped to the table, and again for the third joint. When you arrive at the fourth and final joint, the first piece of moulding will be hovering around the fourth, waiting to be joined, and it will have to be lifted slightly to get the glue brush on to the final mitre.

Remove the assembled frame from the table, check it for flatness and squareness and lay it aside to dry. If the mitres are perfect, it should be flat and square. If not, it might be necessary to twist or 'lozenge' the assembly very slightly to bring it flat and square, though probably at the expense of a gap appearing in one of the corners.

If the mitres are not perfect to start with, or if the practice described above proves difficult, it is best to assemble the frame within a mitring jig. In this case, the first two pieces to be assembled are laid into the jig, again with a smear of woodworking adhesive on one mitre face, and are pushed tightly together. When the joint appears flush and square, the two pieces are clamped up tightly with the jig vice jaws, and the corner pins are driven in. The process is repeated for the other three corners.

Pilot holes for bigger pins can be drilled with the pieces clamped into a mitring jig, using a hand drill or a hand-held power drill, but extra-long drills may have to be employed to reach into the jig. **If the holes are pre-drilled before assembly, a vertical drill press should be used to ensure that the holes are exactly square to the moulding. If they are not, the action of driving in pins that are pushed out of square by angled holes will cause uncontrollable slip in the joint during assembly, and no amount of offset (see Figure 38) will overcome it. Accurate, square-drilled pilot holes overcome slip automatically, because the pin begins to bite immediately driving starts, and no offsetting is necessary during assembly.**

Finishing

A frame made of finished, coloured moulding with accurate mitres needs no finishing except for the touching-up of pin heads and any tiny chips that might appear on the outer edges of the mitres. **Touch-**

ing up is best done with a small brush and model paints, which are available in small tins in most model shops. A collection of basic colours in matt finish, plus black, white and brown, can be mixed together in tiny quantities to give almost any colour that is required to match those of a finished frame, and the touch-up marks are practically invisible when dry.

Unfinished, raw-timber frames need further treatment. First, as explained earlier, excess adhesive that has wept out of the joints must be allowed to half-dry, and it must then be cut away with a sharp blade. Second, if the mitres are not perfect, and gaps are apparent in the joints, these must be filled with plastic wood, preferably in a colour matching that of the raw timber. The plastic wood should protrude from the gaps, and this too should be cut flush with the wood surface just before it goes hard. Attempting to sand it away after hardening will only damage the nearby timber, but a very fine (400 grit) paper can be used to smooth its surface after cutting.

→ The easiest and quickest finish for a raw-timber frame is stain and polish. Wood stain can be bought in a variety of colours from most hardware stores and can be applied by brush or cloth. It runs into the wood quickly and smoothly, leaving no brush marks if a brush is used, and it can be deepened in tone by successive applications. When a satisfactory tone is attained, it need only be finished by wiping on a good-quality wax polish with a soft, lint-free cloth, and rubbing down the polish until a soft gleam appears. Second and third coats of polish, after the previous coats have dried, provide more attractive depth to the finish, which is permanent.

A heavier-duty finish is stain and varnish, but the varnish must be applied from an aerosol can, or it must be thinned down with white spirit so that it flows on to the frame almost as freely as water, with

repeat coats after each has dried. Thick varnish, applied by brush, gives an unappealing, non-professional look to a finished frame.

Painting by brush is equally unappealing. Paint must be applied by aerosol or spray-gun, after the timber has been sealed by a spray varnish or by very thinned-down, watery, brush-on varnish. Once the timber is sealed, any spray-paint will adhere satisfactorily and provide a pleasant finish, including matt, semi-gloss or gloss automobile paints obtainable from car accessory shops. With sufficient patience and care, striped effects can be obtained by laying down a base colour and then masking, with masking tape, to leave strips on to which gold, silver or other colours can be sprayed. After such spray-painting, no further finishing or touching-up is needed.

Mounts and Backing Boards

Marking Off Mounts

For a given size and proportion of picture, the overall dimensions of the mount can be determined from the recommendations given in the section on mount proportions (page 25).

Lay the mount card face down on a clean, flat surface, and mark off its overall length and depth along two adjacent edges, which will be exactly at right angles if it is a new, uncut piece of card. From these marks, draw the two opposing edges, making sure that the drawn lines are exactly at right angles to the card edges. A large set-square, as used by draftsmen, is best for this purpose, with one edge laid along the card edge and the other used to draw the first part of the lines. Continue the lines until they meet to form the complete rectangle, and check it again for accuracy and squareness.

Cut the card to size, using a heavy-duty craft knife,

such as a Stanley knife, with a new, sharp blade, and a rigid steel straight-edge to guide the knife. The best surface to cut on is thick glass, such as that used for table tops, but if this is not available, use thick cardboard or hardboard.

Now mark out the aperture, using if you wish the 'golden ratio' rules (page 25) in which the base of the mount will be a little wider than the top and sides, and prepare for cutting.

Mount Cutting

If the mount card is very thin (less than 1mm) mitre-cutting the aperture (see Figure 2, page 13) is not worth the effort, because the mitre will be practically invisible, and the knife blade can be held vertically while cutting. If the card is thicker, such as the standard '6-sheet' or '10-sheet' found in most artists' suppliers, then mitring is worth while.

→ A successful mitre cut can be made with no more than a good straight-edge and a steady hand. It is best to adopt a cutting angle of 60° (see Figure 39) instead of the machine-cut 45°, because it is very difficult to hold a steady 45° while cutting, whereas a constant 60° can be achieved after a little practice.

Now, with the aperture marked out on the *back* of the card, place down the straight-edge a little distance away from the first line to be cut so that the angled knife will enter the card exactly on the line, as shown in the drawing. Holding the straight-edge very firmly, start the cut a little way beyond the end of the line, and make a first shallow cut along the line, continuing a little beyond its marked end (see Figure 40). The small over-runs at the beginning and end of each line are necessary to ensure a full-cut-out of the aperture, but they must not be taken so far that the excess cutting appears at the front of the mount. A little practice on a scrap piece of mount card will

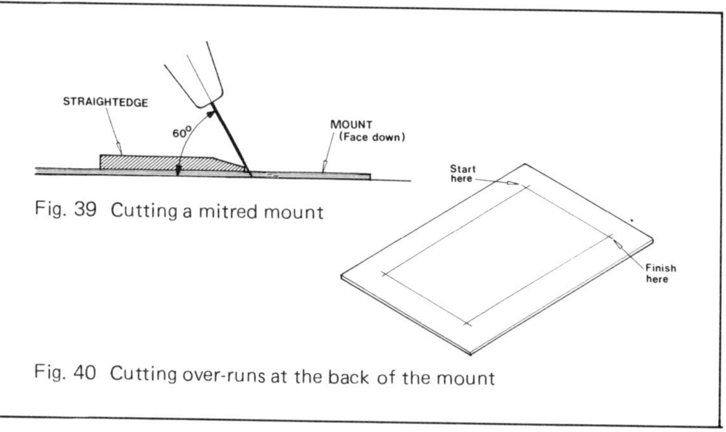

Fig. 39 Cutting a mitred mount

Fig. 40 Cutting over-runs at the back of the mount

quickly show the amount of over-run needed, depending on the cutting angle chosen and also on the manner in which the knife is held in the hand. Typically, for mount card 1.5mm (1/16 in) thick, an over-run of 3mm (1/8 in) at each end will provide a perfect mitred corner with no evidence of over-cutting on the front face.

If you find it difficult to hold the straight-edge firmly enough for a long cut – this does require very heavy hand-pressure – clamp the straight-edge down on to the mount using G-clamps, positioned so that they do not interfere with the cut.

Continue cutting lightly from end to end of the line, including the over-runs, maintaining the cutting angle as closely as possible, until the blade is felt to have cut through the card. This is where cutting on glass has an advantage, because the blade will suddenly slip cleanly through the cut without more effort, and glass prevents a slight 'burr' being raised on the front face of the mount.

Repeat the cutting process on the other three sides of the aperture and then turn the card over to examine the cuts on the front face. If they have been completed fully, they will appear as a fully completed

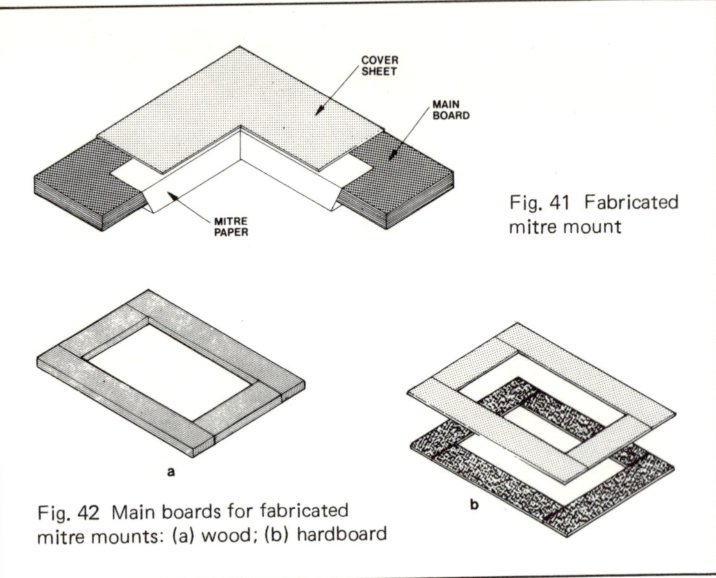

Fig. 41 Fabricated mitre mount

Fig. 42 Main boards for fabricated mitre mounts: (a) wood; (b) hardboard

rectangle, and the centre can be simply pushed out from behind, leaving a clean-cut mitred mount. If the cutting is incomplete, and the centre remains stuck, check where the edges have to be cut farther, turn the card face down again, and gently complete the missing cuts, maintaining the original cutting angle and avoiding cutting beyond the original over-run limits.

→ **With sufficient practice, angle-cutting a mount card from the rear face in this manner will always produce a perfect mitred mount that will stand up to the closest of inspections.**

Fabricated Mitre Mounts

Very attractive two-colour mitred mounts can be made at home without resorting to angled cutting of mount boards and, because they can be much thicker than standard boards, they present an expensive-looking appearance for very little cost.

The mitres are made of folded paper strips stuck to a thick board and covered with a thin paper sheet of another colour, as shown in Figure 41, and the procedure for making these mounts is as follows.

The main mount board can be made of thick cardboard, hardboard or wood. With cardboard, it is easiest to cut the mount as one piece, using a Stanley knife and a steel straight-edge, without bothering about cutting over-runs at the corners of the aperture, because they will not be seen again. With hardboard, it is best to use strips cut to the mount width, assembled as shown in Figure 42, with the rough faces glued together. Here, each butt joint is supported by the pieces of the opposing half. With wood, glued butt joints, also shown in Figure 42, are adequate.

The mitres can be made from any good-quality white or coloured paper, such as poster paper, and Figure 43 shows the shape to which they are cut and scored. After cutting out, the strips are folded along the score lines and are glued to the mount board as

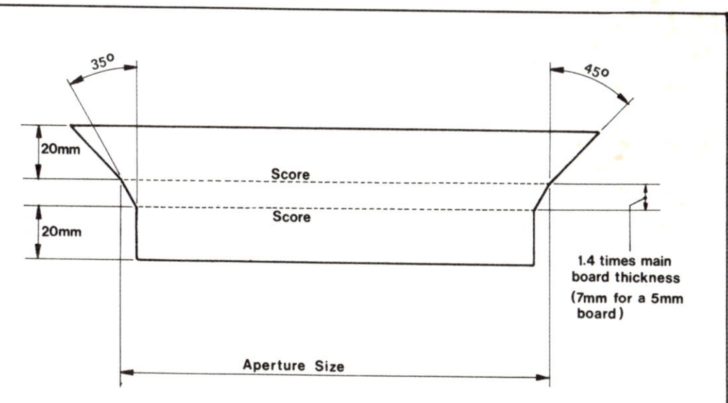

Fig. 43 Dimensions for cutting and scoring paper strips for a fabricated mitre mount

shown in Figure 44, with the central section of each strip sloping down at 45°. The width of the central section (1.4 times the board thickness) ensures that this angle is achieved automatically when the two outer sections are glued flat to the board without bending the paper. The 35° angles at the ends of the strips also ensure that the mitre ends match properly, and these ends may be touched with a little glue from behind to hold them together.

Finally, the cover sheet, also made from good-quality paper, in a contrasting or matching colour, is cut and glued to the front of the assembly. Its aperture is cut a fraction larger than that of the main board (say 1 or 2mm all round) so that a thin stripe of the mitre paper can be seen inside the cover sheet aperture, as shown in Figure 41.

Remember, when deciding the size of the main board aperture, that the paper mitres will reduce the size of the final aperture by the thickness of the main board all round, and that the main board aperture should be enlarged accordingly.

Backing Boards

Backing boards should be as stiff as possible while being thin enough to ensure that there is adequate depth in the frame moulding rebate to accept the entire sandwich of glass, mount, picture and board (see Figure 45).

If sufficient rebate depth is available, the best material to use is 3-mm (⅛-in) hardboard, machine-sawn to the size of the mount and sanded on all edges. If a machine saw is not available, most hardware shops will cut hardboard to the size required. If there is unsufficient rebate depth, 2-mm cardboard may be used as a backing board, cut to size with a Stanley knife, but this is the minimum thickness for → pictures up to 50cm (20in) in length. **Any backing**

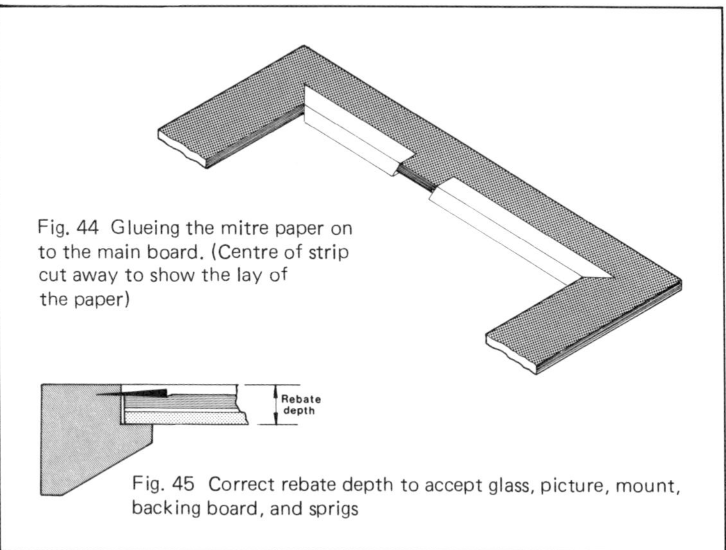

Fig. 44 Glueing the mitre paper on to the main board. (Centre of strip cut away to show the lay of the paper)

Fig. 45 Correct rebate depth to accept glass, picture, mount, backing board, and sprigs

board below that thickness will be totally inadequate as a stiffener, and if the sandwich, with a 2-mm backing board, cannot be accommodated in the rebate, a larger frame moulding, with a deeper rebate, must be used.

For pictures between 50cm (20in) and 1 metre (3ft) in length, 3-mm hardboard or thicker board must be used. For pictures over 1 metre in length, the backing board must be made of plywood at least 6mm (¼in) thick.

Glass

Glass Thickness

The thinnest glass that is readily available from most suppliers is about 2mm thick, and it is suitable for pictures up to 50cm (20in) in length. For larger pictures, 3-mm glass should be used.

2-mm glass is unnecessarily thick for smaller pictures – below 25cm (10in) in length – where

1-mm sheet is adequate, but these thinner glasses are very difficult to obtain now. They can be found in old frames, however, and if an old frame is scrapped the glass should be kept, wrapped in several sheets of newspaper for safe storage, for cutting to a new size later. These thinner glasses are very easy to cut.

Glass Cutting

For framing one or two pictures, the quickest, easiest and cheapest way of getting a piece of glass of the right size is to have it cut by a local glass supplier. He bears the cost of mistakes, breakages, tools, cutting tables and glass stocks. When ordering the glass, specify the thickness needed, and remember the clearance required between the glass and the frame (see the section on measuring, page 34) if the frame has already been made. The supplier will normally cut to an accuracy of 1mm (1/32 in).

If many pictures are to be framed, and particularly if stocks of glass from old frames are available, then it does become more economic to cut your own glass.

Cutting glass can be a frustrating and disappointing (and expensive) process unless you have the right equipment and you follow a few tricks of the trade. You need:

A *flat* table, large enough to accommodate the uncut sheet.

A thick, steel straight-edge, longer than the longest dimension of the uncut glass. A professional straight-edge is best, but a length of mild steel bar or angle, available from well-stocked hardware stores, will do.

A measuring rule.

A glass-marking pencil or felt-tipped pen.

A piece of old blanket to cover the table.

A glass-cutting tool.

It is, of course, the last item that can make or, literally, break the job. It must be *sharp*. The professional glazier sharpens his cutting wheel at the end of each day's work, but this is beyond the capability of most of us. Be prepared, therefore, to buy a new tool and to throw away any old glass-cutting tools whose history you do not know. They will cost more in broken glass than the price of a new one. The best type to buy is that with five or six numbered cutting wheels set into a rotating head. Start with no.1 wheel, and use it for not more than 10m (30ft) of cutting, keeping a record of the length of cuts. Then change to no.2 wheel, and so on until all six wheels are used up. That will cover a lot of pictures.

To cut the glass, proceed as follows. Lay the un-cut glass on the blanket-covered table. Check that two adjacent edges are dead square (they should be if it is a new piece of glass or a piece from an old frame) by laying a 90° try-square at the corner. If they are not, draw a line at right-angles to one of the edges, using the try-square and the glass marker, and draw this line at least 5cm (2in) from the un-square edge, because this is going to be one of the cuts.

Using either the ready-squared edges, or one edge and the newly drawn line, lay out the rectangular shape to be cut, measuring as carefully as possible, and checking for squareness with a draftsman's set-square.

When you are satisfied that the dimensions are correct, and that no cutting line falls less than 5cm (2in) from an uncut edge, you are ready to begin cutting.

Lay the straight-edge near the first line to be cut so that the larger of the two pieces, after cutting, will be on your left (if you are right-handed). Bring the straight-edge up to the line, from the left, leaving a clearance so that the cutting wheel will fall on the line itself. With most glass-cutting tools, this clearance is 3mm (⅛ in).

→ **Now, holding the straight-edge** *very firmly* **with your left hand, lay the cutting wheel on to the glass and draw it down the straight-edge** *using no more pressure than you would with a ball-point pen on a*
→ *sheet of paper*. **If you have the right pressure, there should be no more than the faintest 'hiss' as the wheel runs down the glass, leaving behind it a faint grey line. Crackling noises reveal excessive pressure, or a blunt wheel, either of which will ruin the cut.**

Lift up the glass, and slide the straight-edge under it, lining up the straight-edge so that its right-hand edge lies directly under the line, with the piece to be broken off sticking up in the air a little, above the surface of the blanket. Holding the main (left) piece firmly with your left hand, place the palm of your right hand half-way along the right-hand piece and push gently. The right-hand piece will snap off instantly and cleanly.

Repeat for the other edges.

Note that, to ensure a clean snap, the right-hand piece should not be less than 5cm (2in) wide. Narrower strips might prove difficult except on very thin (1-mm) sheets.

On occasion, despite every care, the break line may run away from the drawn line towards the end of the cut. If the run-off is inwards, that is, into the final rectangle, the piece must be discarded and used later for a smaller picture. If the run-off is outwards, it can be corrected by gently bending the excess piece downwards, either with pliers or with the slots found in most glass-cutting tools, and it will break away, still leaving a small excess pinnacle of glass. This pinnacle might be small enough to fall within the glass-frame clearance already allowed for in measuring, and may be left. If not, it itself may be gently broken away with the nose of a pair of pliers, until there is simply an uneven section of line left. In all such attempts at correction, glass fragments will fly, so *wear goggles or spectacles.*

Glass Cleaning

The glass is cleaned in two stages, first wet, before picture assembly, and then dry, during and after assembly. The second stage is described in the section on assembly (page 60) and here we consider only initial wet cleaning.

The sheet of glass is held in a sink, or washing-up bowl, filled with warm water and a little washing-up liquid. As with any household glassware, rub the warm water over both surfaces of the glass, using a dish cloth, turning the glass when necessary to get all of it under water. When it is clearly free of dirt and greasy marks, take it out and stand it up to drain. When it is dry, or nearly dry, lay it on a clean tea towel, and buff the upper surface lightly with another clean tea towel. Using the second towel to prevent your fingers touching the glass, turn it over and buff the other side. Still holding it in a towel, lift it up and lightly dust off bits of lint until it is gleamingly clean. Wrap it in a sheet of newspaper, ready for assembly.

Picture Preparation

All the work described so far, and all the work yet to come, is for the benefit of one component, the picture itself, and now *it* must be prepared for framing. The preparation consists of two processes: trimming it to size, and bonding it or preparing it for hanging within the frame.

Trimming

Trimming might be required for two reasons:

1. The finished frame is slightly undersized, and the picture, if it is not mounted, needs to be cut down slightly to the size of the glass, to give the same clearance.

2. The picture, particularly if it is a print, may have an excessively wide border which does not suit the dimensions chosen for the mount or the frame.

In either case, trimming is accomplished by drawing light pencil lines at the required distances from the picture edges, and cutting through those lines with a sharp craft knife and a steel straight-edge. Again, a sheet of glass is the best material to cut on (see the section on mounts, page 47), and the straight-edge should be laid on a clean piece of paper to ensure that it does not mark the picture.

Bonding

As explained in Part One of this book, a light-weight picture will buckle within a frame unless it has been bonded to a stiff support sheet, but the home picture framer does not have access to the big hot-bonding presses of the professional.

There are two ways of overcoming this problem. The first is simply to 'hang' the picture within the frame, if it appears adequately stiff in itself, and the second is to use bonding techniques that can be accomplished in the home.

'Hanging' the picture consists simply of attaching it to the back of the mount with two short pieces of clear adhesive tape near the top corners of the picture. → **A long strip of tape must not be used, nor should any other pieces be placed at the sides or at the bottom, because differential expansion and contraction between the mount and the picture will inevitably lead to ugly buckling gaps appearing between the** two. This system can work only if the picture itself is already mounted or painted on thin card, such as Bristol board, or on very heavy-weight water-colour paper. If it is thinner, and particularly if it is a paper print or a photograph, internal hanging simply will not do, as the resultant waves and gaps between picture and mount, or picture and frame, are offensive to the eye. A form of bonding must be applied.

Two bonding processes can be used – dry or wet – and each has its advantages and disadvantages.

Dry bonding is the better of the two, but it is the more expensive. It uses double-sided adhesive sheet, available from well-stocked artists' and drawing-office suppliers, which comes in rolls or large sheets that can be cut to size. The protective paper on one side is pulled off, and the sheet is carefully smoothed down on to the backing board and trimmed to size. Then the front protective paper is peeled off, and the picture is carefully smoothed down on to the sheet. Great care must be taken to ensure that the picture is lined up properly, because once it is down it can never be lifted again.

Being a dry process, this system cannot cause staining of any type of picture, and the bonding sheet effectively protects the picture from staining chemicals that might be present in the backing board, which is not the case with wet bonding.

Wet bonding can be achieved satisfactorily only ← with spray adhesive. Glues in bottles or tubes cannot be laid down with sufficient control of thickness to achieve a perfectly flat finish, and many of them can 'weep' chemicals through the picture, staining it permanently. But spray adhesive has its problems too, which can be overcome by following a few guide lines.

First, unless the backing board is known to be of ← picture-framing quality, the picture must not be bonded down to it with spray adhesive. The professional framer specifies the maximum acid and other chemical content of the hardboard that he uses for backing, to avoid staining problems, but commercial hardboard from a builders' supplier does not meet these requirements. Nor do most sheets of cardboard. The picture must therefore be bonded down to a stiffening sheet that is known to be free of staining chemicals, and this can apply only to Bristol board or to very heavy-quality white cartridge paper of at least 200 grammes per square metre in weight. For small pictures, white poster card, or white folders, available in stationer's shops, are satisfactory for the purpose.

The white stiffening sheet should be left over-size before bonding, so that the picture can be laid on to it without your worrying about exact positioning. The picture is held vertically, preferably by a pair of large tweezers, and the spray adhesive is applied to the back of the picture, following the instructions on the spray can. When the surface is totally covered with a thin, almost invisible layer of adhesive, it is laid on to the stiffener and smoothed flat. The stiffener is then trimmed back to the size of the picture.

Note: Spray adhesives are dangerous. They are inflammable and contain chemicals that must not be inhaled. Use them only in a well-ventilated room.

Assembly and Finishing

Insertion and Staking

The first stage in assembly is to insert the glass/

mount/picture/backing board sandwich into the frame and to stake it in place.

Place the frame, front-down, on a piece of old blanket, unwrap the clean glass, and lay it into the frame. If there are any signs of dirt or grease on the glass, clean its inside face now, using a dry-cleaning process. **This simply involves rubbing over the face lightly with a very fine (400-grit) piece of glasspaper, wrapped around a small block of wood, which effectively removes the last traces of dirt without leaving moisture in the frame.**

Now lay down the stiffened picture, or the stiffened picture stuck to its mount with a couple of pieces of adhesive tape, followed by the backing board.

Holding the whole assembly together, turn it face up and look very carefully for specks of dust, lint, or sawdust that might be lying under the glass. If any are visible, turn the picture over again, take out the backing board and picture, and remove the specks from the glass or the mount or picture. *Don't rub the glass to remove them.* **Glass, being an insulator, becomes electrostatically charged when rubbed and attracts more dust, and you will be rubbing and re-cleaning for ever. Put back the picture and backing board, and check once more for dust. If all is clear, you are ready to stake. If not, clean again, because this is your last chance to get in between the glass and the picture.**

Staking is accomplished by driving small steel 'sprigs' into the inside edges of the rebate, and the rebate depth must be enough to accommodate the whole picture/glass sandwich with not less than 2mm ($^{1}/_{16}$ in) to spare to take the sprigs (see Figure 45, page 53). This is one of the criteria to watch when choosing your moulding.

The professional framer uses flat steel sprigs

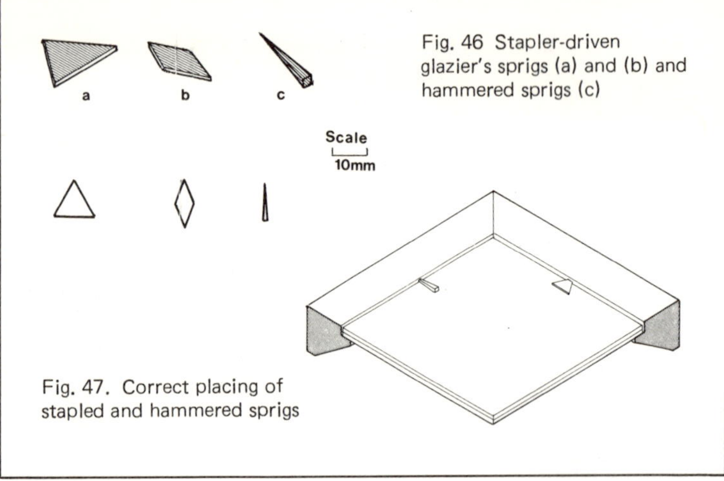

Fig. 46 Stapler-driven glazier's sprigs (a) and (b) and hammered sprigs (c)

Fig. 47. Correct placing of stapled and hammered sprigs

(Figure 46, a and b) driven in by a glazier's stapler, so that they trap the sandwich as shown in Figure 47. Without this specialist tool, the home framer must use traditional sprigs, of the type shown in Figure 46c, driven in with a pin hammer. **Do not use moulding pins or panel pins for staking because, not being tapered like the sprig, they do not align themselves when driving in to bite down into the backing board, as seen in Figure 45. A correctly driven sprig is shown in Figure 47, and the way it is driven is shown in Figure 48. Here, with the picture face-down on a piece of protective blanket, the frame side is pushed up against a block of wood clamped to the workbench, so that the shock of pin-driving is taken out in the block. Starting at the centre of one of the long sides, place a sprig against the inside of the frame moulding, as shown in the drawing, press down on the glass/picture sandwich, and gently tap the sprig into the moulding, using a pin hammer sliding across the surface of the backing board. The sprig should be driven in to about one-third of its length.**

The spacing and number of sprigs depends on the

size of the picture. A typical spacing is 5cm (2in) and the consequent layout of sprigs for a picture of 25cm x 15cm (10in x 6in) is shown in Figure 49, which also shows the recommended order of sprig insertion.

Sealing

The back of the frame must be sealed to prevent ingress of dust, mites and moisture, and this is accomplished by laying down strips of self- or wet adhesive tape, as shown in Figure 50. The tape should be pressed firmly on to the backing board and the frame, and should be trimmed so that it lies neatly clear of the frame edge all the way round.

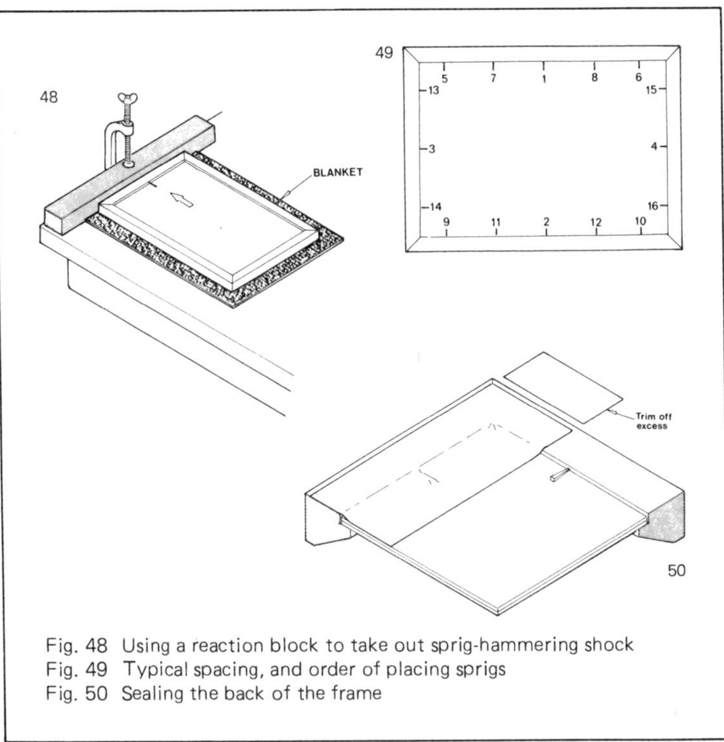

Fig. 48 Using a reaction block to take out sprig-hammering shock
Fig. 49 Typical spacing, and order of placing sprigs
Fig. 50 Sealing the back of the frame

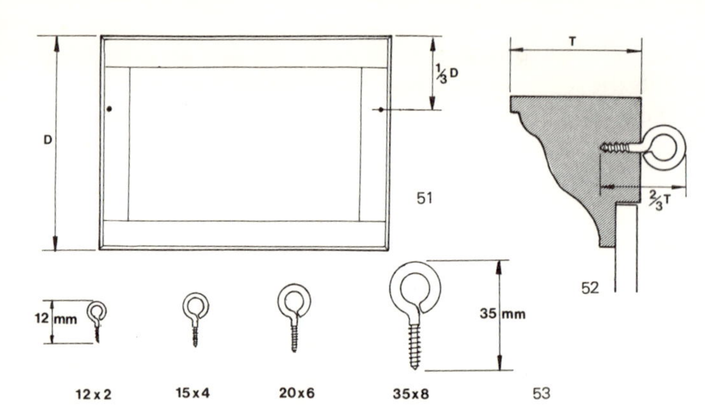

Fig. 51 Positioning hanging eyes
Fig. 52 Correct proportion for a hanging eye
Fig. 53 Typical examples of hanging eyes and their size designations. The first number represents overall length and the second the wood screw size

Hanging Eyes

The general position for hanging eyes is seen in Figure 51, which shows that they should be placed one-third of the way down the vertical sides of the picture. Pilot holes, drilled with a hand or power drill, or bored with a bradawl, need to be made at these positions, and the size of the holes depends on the size of the hanging eyes, which in turn depend on the size of the frame moulding itself. Figure 52 shows the generally accepted rule for eye sizes, which are always dimensioned by their overall length. **The length should be two-thirds of the thickness of the frame moulding, with the eye screwed in until the circular part touches the wood.**

Eyes are available in a range of sizes, some of which are shown in Figure 53, and the nearest standard size should be chosen to meet the length criterion shown in Figure 52. Thus, for a frame moulding of 30-mm thickness, a 20-mm eye should be chosen. For 20-mm thickness, a 15-mm eye should be used, it being better to aim on the high side when selecting the length nearest to the optimum.

It will be seen from Figure 53 that length and screw size are generally related to each other. Thus a 15-mm eye normally has a size 4 screw, while a 35-mm eye takes a size 8 screw. These screw sizes are the same as those used for standard woodworking screws, and thus use the same size of pilot holes when working in hardwood. Standard pilot hole sizes are:

SCREW SIZE	PILOT DRILL	
	mm	in
2	1	$\frac{3}{64}$
4	2	$\frac{5}{64}$
6	2.5	$\frac{3}{32}$
8	3	$\frac{7}{64}$

It is far better to drill a pilot hole than to bore it with a bradawl, whatever its size, because a drilled hole gives a clean, straight and safe start to the screw thread. From size 6 upwards, boring can split the moulding, and a drill must be used. ←

A working figure for the average weight of framed pictures is 2 lb per square foot. (Here we will stay with imperial measures for the moment.) Thus, a picture measuring 36in x 30in (7½ sq ft) will weigh about 15 lb, and a picture 24in x 12in (2 sq ft) will weigh about 4 lb. **To carry the 15-lb weight safely, two 35-mm eyes should be used, and this implies a frame thickness of 50mm (2in) with an equivalent width when viewed from the front – that is, about 50mm also, as recommended in Part One.** ← The smaller picture needs two 15-mm eyes, with a consequent frame size of about 1in x 1in. The table below shows the approximate weight and typical size of framed pictures that can be hung safely on the sizes of eyes shown.

EYE SIZE	PICTURE WEIGHT		TYPICAL SIZE	
	kg	lb	cm	in
35 x 8	7	15	90 x 75	36 x 30
20 x 6	4.5	10	75 x 60	30 x 24
15 x 4	2	5	60 x 37	24 x 15
12 x 2	0.5	1	30 x 15	12 x 6

Hangers for Thin Frames

Sometimes, for reasons of economy, or because an old frame is already available, the frame-moulding thickness and width fall way below the recommendations given for aesthetic and structural reasons. **While appearance is a matter of personal taste, structural strength affects the safety not only of the picture itself, but also of anyone who might be near a picture that might fall off a wall.**

Thin frames fitted to large pictures cannot accept the recommended sizes of hanging eyes for the size and weight of the pictures, and a different hanging system has to be adopted. This is shown in Figure 54, where it will be seen that the hanging points are transferred to the backing board, using a different form of hanger known as a 'D-ring', which is shown in more detail in Figure 55c.

For this method of hanging pictures up to 2kg (5lb) in weight, 3-mm hardboard is the thinnest backing board which should be used. Above that weight, 6-mm (¼-inch) plywood must be used. D-rings cannot be fitted satisfactorily to cardboard.

Up to the 2-kg limit, one D-ring, centred near the top of the picture, is adequate. Beyond that limit, two should be fitted, angled inwards as shown in Figure 54, to line up with the hanging cord when it is fitted later.

D-rings should be fitted to the backing board with bifurcated rivets, of the type shown in Figure 56. These can be hammered flat, as shown in the drawing,

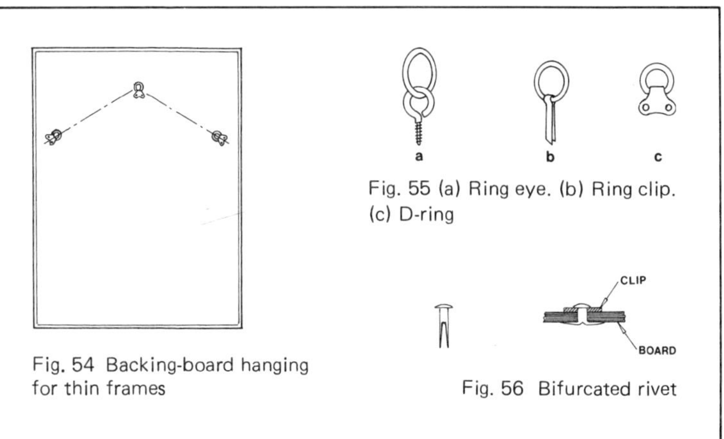

Fig. 54 Backing-board hanging for thin frames

Fig. 55 (a) Ring eye. (b) Ring clip. (c) D-ring

Fig. 56 Bifurcated rivet

after they have been passed through the metal hanger and the backing board, so that they do not produce bumps under the picture.

In this type of hanging, it is important to ensure that the glass/picture/board sandwich is pressed tightly into the frame while staking and that an extra number of sprigs is used, so that the sandwich and frame form a tight assembly. If not, the weight of the glass will tend to push the frame forwards, away from the backing board which is taking the load, unlike a full-sized frame, which takes the load itself through its side members.

For very small and light pictures with thin frames, D-rings can be replaced by lightweight ring clips, of the form shown in Figure 55b. This drawing also shows a ring eye (a), which can be used for single-eye hanging of a small picture by inserting it at the centre of the top member of the frame, and slipping the ring over a hook or nail, but this is rather unsightly. Ring eyes can also be used in place of normal eyes, having the advantage, at slightly increased cost, of hiding the hanging cord completely, because the rings pull inwards behind the frame.

Finishing

With the hanging eyes fitted, all that remains to finish the framed picture is to clean it, and to touch up any damage that may have occurred to the frame. Touching up is described on page 45. **The front of the glass should be cleaned with the 400-grit paper used for the inside face (see page 61), and the whole picture wiped over with a soft cloth.** Finally there is the fitting of the cord – for this procedure see page 82 in Part Three.

Exhibition and Display Frames

Simple exhibition and display frames, of the types shown in Figures 13 and 14, can be made very easily in the home, it being necessary only to cut the backing boards and glass, or have them cut, and to supply the clips. **Remember, however, that the glass edges are exposed on these frames, and that they must be ground smooth by the glass supplier.**

Passe-Partout

The non-availability, nowadays, of passe-partout framing tape has been mentioned in Part One (see page 23) but this does not prevent the home framer from producing an attractive passe-partout frame at very little cost. Moreover, if the hardboard back and the glass can be supplied cut to size, the only tools needed are a steel rule, a Stanley knife and a bradawl.

The process is shown in Figure 57 but, before going through the steps, note the following limitations. **The maximum picture size that can be framed is 25-cm (10-in) square. Above this size, the glass may slip in the tape. The picture must be bonded down on to suitable stiff card (see the section on bonding, page 58) to prevent it buckling under the glass.**

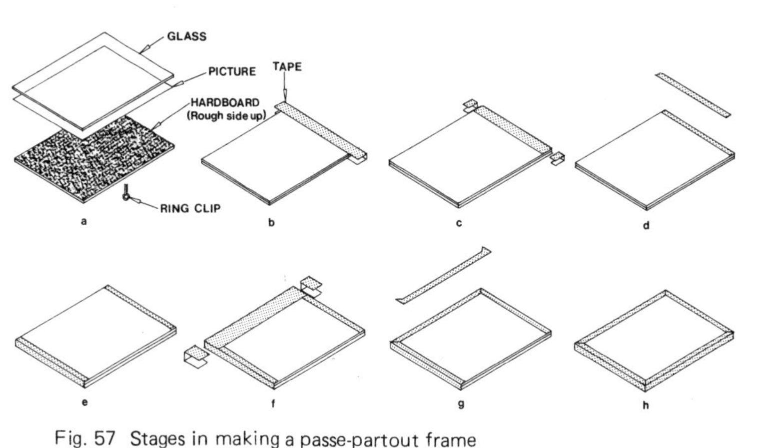

Fig. 57 Stages in making a passe-partout frame

This need to bond down may be used to advantage to produce a very cheap mount effect. The mount may be made of coloured poster paper (or white paper if the picture is dark-toned) cut to a size larger than the picture, using the size recommendations shown for mounts in Part One (page 25). Then, using a spray adhesive as described on page 59, the picture is bonded in place on top of the mount. It is often easier to bond down the picture first and then cut the mount to size afterwards. Now bonded, with or without an exposed mount, the picture is ready for framing.

Cut to size, or have cut to size, the glass and the 3-mm hardboard backing board to the dimensions of the picture or its larger mount. Mark a central point near the top of the hardboard, and here drill or bore a hole big enough (about 3mm or ⅛ in) to take the arms of a ring clip.

Assemble the parts as shown in Figure 57a, with the rough side of the hardboard facing up, push the arms of the ring clip through the hole from below, open them up and press them flat. Press the glass, picture and hardboard together to make a thin sandwich, and prepare to tape.

The best tape to use is carpet tape – available in a wide range of colours and widths from most hardware stores – with a slightly stippled finish that gives a pleasing appearance to the frame. A tape width of 5cm (2in) is adequate, but wider tape may be used, at the expense of more waste.

Cut a piece of tape slightly longer than the top of the picture, and peel off the protective backing sheet. Lay it down over the top edge so that about 1cm (½in) is covering the glass and press this width firmly on to the glass. Accuracy in placing is not necessary, either in width or in parallelism to the glass edge, because you are going to trim it straight later. Now fold the tape over the edge of the sandwich, pressing it flat against the edge, and then again on to the smooth hardboard face at the rear, smoothing and pressing all along the length and making sure that the bent corners are tight and square (see Figure 57b). With a very sharp blade, preferably brand new, trim off the excess tape as shown in Figure 57c.

Now, depending on the 'straightness' of your eye you can either trim off directly or mark off for trimming. To mark off, draw a pencil line 6mm (¼in) from the edge, and lay the steel rule against it; or simply lay the rule at an estimated distance, parallel with the edge. Holding the rule firmly, draw the blade along it, cutting into the tape, and then peel the excess tape away (see Figure 57d). Repeat at the other end (Figure 57e).

Next, lay, fold and press down another piece of tape along one of the sides, again not bothering with accuracy in laying, and trim off the excess at each end, taking care this time not to cut into the earlier pieces of tape that are already there (Figure 57f).

At this stage, simple trimming-off the excess width

is not good enough, because the tape joints must be mitred. Again draw a line at 6mm (¼in) from the edge, but at the ends draw two small lines at 45° (which can be estimated by eye) running to the corners of the picture. Cut these two lines first, from the face of the picture towards the corners. Now, with the steel rule laid firmly down at its 6mm from the edge, cut along the tape between the two 45° cuts, and peel away the piece shown in Figure 57g. (Here, because there is a tiny triangle of top and bottom tape lying under the ends of the newly cut side tape, the perfectionist lifts the ends and peels out the triangles, but this is not really necessary.)

Repeat on the other side (Figure 57h), and the picture is ready to hang.

The glass should be clean (see page 00) before taping, to ensure that the tape adheres well, and the tape must be pressed very firmly into place at the front and the back if it is not to fail later under the weight of the glass.

Tools and Jigs

A list of tools and jigs, with alternatives, required for the making of 'classic' frames in the home, and classified in relation to the various procedures required, is given below. For exhibition and display frames, and for passe-partout work, with glass and backing boards cut to size by a supplier, you need only a steel rule, a Stanley knife, a bradawl, and perhaps a screwdriver to fix hanging rings or clips to boards.

FOR MEASURING AND MARKING OUT	3-ft or 1-m folding rule 3-ft or 1-m steel straight-edge 1-ft or 30-cm steel rule

FOR MEASURING AND MARKING OUT *(continued)*	Draftsman's 45° set-square Carpenter's 90° try-square Carpenter's 45° try-square Slide calipers (for drill sizes)
FOR CUTTING MOULDINGS	By machine: Bench saw or bandsaw with tilt tables By hand: 45° mitring jig (see Figure 30, page 37) or fine-tooth tenon saw
FOR MAKING UP FRAMES	Rotary or belt sander with tilt table or sanding jig (see Figure 31, page 39) or planing jig (see Figure 32, page 40) Pin hammer Hand drill or power drill Bradawl G-clamps Mitring jig or clamping jig (see Figure 34, page 41) Pliers Screwdrivers
FOR GLASS CUTTING	Multi-wheel glass cutter
FOR CUTTING MOUNTS AND TAPES	Stanley knife, or equivalent, with renewable blades
FOR HANGING	Builder's level, or water tube (see Figure 68, page 86) Large hammer

Using and Renovating Old Frames

Frames in Good Condition

The cheapest way of framing a picture is to use an old frame in good condition. If it fits the proportions of the picture, or if it is clear that a picture mount can be inserted to accommodate a small picture in an over-size frame (see the section on frame and mount sizes on page 24), it is only necessary to remove the original picture and put in the new one.

To remove the original, cut through the sealing tape at the back of the frame, and peel it away to expose the staking sprigs. Work these out of the frame moulding by pushing them sideways, in both directions, until they fall free, and lay them aside. Take out the backing board, picture and mount, and remove the glass for cleaning. Then, using the processes described in the preceding pages, prepare the new picture and mount for framing. Re-insert the glass, picture and backing board, taking care to check for dust as described on page 61, and, **if the sandwich thickness is the same as the original and glazier's flat sprigs have been used, push them back into their original slits, pressing them in hard with a heavy screwdriver blade. If the new sandwich is too thick, or if ordinary sprigs were used, re-stake with new sprigs, following the procedure described on page 61.** Remove the hanging eyes, re-seal with new tape, and re-insert the eyes.

This procedure should be followed when there is simply a need to replace a broken glass in an existing picture.

Damaged Frames

The most common damage that is seen in old frames is the opening of one or more of the mitred corners. Even if only one joint appears to be open, it is unlikely that the other three are unaffected, because the damage is probably the result of physical 'lozenging' of the frame or of damp, either of which will affect all the joints. If, however, examination of the frame reveals that only one joint is damaged and that the other three are tight and stiff, it is worth attempting a repair to the damaged joint only.

Clean out any dirt in the joint with a small brush, and check to see that the mitres can be brought together neatly under pressure. If they can, without being diverted by bent pins in the joint, mix up some two-part epoxy adhesive and apply it to the joint surfaces with a small spatula. **PVA woodworking adhesive should not be used here, because it cannot bond properly on to old dried glue.** Clamp up the required joint on a belt cramp (see Figure 34, page 41) or in a mitring jig (see Figure 30, page 37) and leave it to set. With large mouldings, of 40mm (1½in) width and above, a repair plate (see Figure 58) can be used to hold a joint together without re-glueing, but a glued joint is always to be recommended.

If the joint will not slide together cleanly and if, as is most likely, all the other joints show signs of weakness, the only thing to do is to dismantle the frame and rebuild it.

To dismantle, pull and twist gently at each joint until the frame members part, taking care not to damage the sharp ends of the mitres. As the locking pins come into view, insert the tip ends of a pair of needle-nose pliers into the joint and *push* the pins out of the mouldings. As their heads come clear of the surface, *pull* them out with a larger pair of pliers.

You now have four mitred pieces of frame moulding, and the next stage depends on their condition. If the wood is undamaged and the finish is satisfactory, you need only prepare the mitre ends for re-jointing, **but this does entail sanding them back, as accurately**

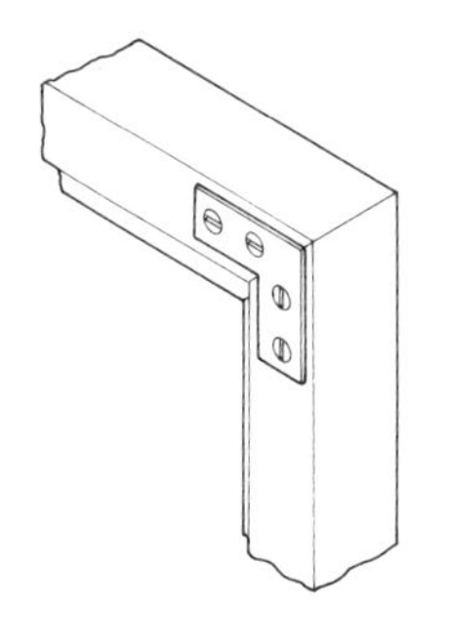

Fig. 58 Repair plate for a large moulding

as if you were making a new frame, using a sanding jig (see Figure 31, page 39) or a planing jig (see Figure 32, page 41). This sanding or planing is essential to ensure effective glueing of the new joints. Hand sanding should not be attempted because it invariably results in slightly curved surfaces, which will wreck the mitres. Jig sanding or planing will remove a fraction of a millimetre at each mitre, and you must check that newly sanded opposing sides are exactly the same length. The frame is then re-assembled following the procedure given on page 40, but new moulding pins must be driven into new locations at each corner, with the original pin holes filled with plastic wood for subsequent touching up.

If the wood itself and the paintwork are damaged, the dismembered frame provides an excellent opportunity to repair and to clean up each of the frame members without worrying about getting into corners. Strip the finish off each member with a chemical paint stripper, or with a soft-mounted rotary sander if the shape is simple and flat. Chemical paint stripper must be removed with a water-soaked rag, and wetting should be kept to a minimum, after which the member should be left to dry completely.

Fill chips and holes with plastic wood or Polyfilla,

and sand back when dry. Re-sand the mitres, as described above, and re-assemble the frame as explained on page 40. Then re-finish the complete frame following the procedure shown on page 45.

Plaster-Covered Frames

Plaster-covered frames, such as those used for old oil paintings, present a more daunting repair job, because areas of damaged plaster must be replaced with new castings taken from other parts of the frame. Normally, these frames are symmetrical in pattern so that if, say, the bottom right-hand corner is damaged, a replacement casting may be taken from the top left corner.

Castings are made by covering the area to be copied with oil (cooking oil will do) and then pressing on to it, firmly and carefully, a large lump of Plasticene that has been worked and warmed to make it soft. When the Plasticene is cool, it is carefully lifted off, the oil preventing it sticking to the plaster, and the resulting mould is then filled with a fine plaster mix, with sufficient water in the mix to make it flow easily. As the mix dries, it sinks in the middle, and this depression is filled with more mix until the surface is flat when dry. The Plasticene is then peeled away from the moulding.

The damaged area on the frame is then rasped and sanded away until a flat, level surface is obtained, and the sides of this surface are squared off. The back of the new moulding is then also rasped and sanded flat, and its edges cut away, until it sits and mates accurately with the surrounding plaster. A little more wet plaster is made up to act as an adhesive and a filler for the joints, the new moulding is set in place, the joints are filled, and the whole frame is left to dry.

After drying, the oil and old paint are removed with chemical stripper, the frame is washed and dried again, and the whole surface is re-finished. This may be done with a single colour, such as dull gold or, to give an 'antique' finish, with gold, grey and red paint. The gold is sprayed down first, followed by grey, which is wiped off while wet to leave grey in the crevices. Then touches of red are applied to some of the plaster pinnacles. If slow-drying, brushed oil paint is used instead of spray paint, the surface may be further treated by baking, to produce fine cracks in the new paint. This is called 'distressing' the finish.

The plaster repair process can also be applied to machine-routed mouldings in which raised patterns, of simpler shape, have been produced on wood.

Part Three

Hanging Pictures

Placing and Grouping Pictures

Over the mantelpiece is the favourite place for the favourite picture, and a very good place it is, too. But when it comes to other pictures and other walls, the choice of hanging places becomes more difficult.

First, access has to be considered. If the picture is a fine, detailed drawing, it is pointless to place it where furniture prevents the viewer from getting a close look at it. But a bold design can be placed high up above a doorway, where it can be enjoyed just as much as if it were at eye level.

Second, lighting must be taken into account. The perfect lighting for viewing pictures is diffused light covering the entire ceiling, but this is found only in some galleries, not at home. So, account must be taken of the position of windows and the direction of sunlight through them. **Unless a frame is fitted with non-reflecting glass (see page 19), or has no glass at all, it is unwise to place it opposite a large, bright window, and no picture should be hung so that it is exposed to long periods of direct sunlight, which can affect the colour of the mount and even of the painting itself.** At night, artificial lighting has to be considered, and this is examined in more detail on page 90.

Third, and most important, there is the question of where to place pictures in relation to others. Often, when starting a collection of pictures, it is

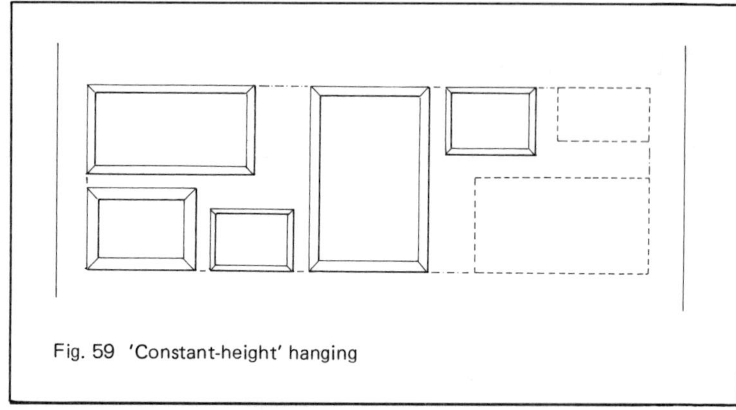
Fig. 59 'Constant-height' hanging

decided to put one picture on each of the four walls of the room 'to spread them out a bit', but this leaves them looking very lonely and sad. It is far better to group them together, at the expense of leaving other walls blank for later acquisitions, because grouping enhances the presentation of pictures and even the pictures themselves.

There are two main methods of grouping, shown in Figures 59 and 60. The first, known as 'constant-level' or 'constant-height' hanging, which is often adopted in exhibitions, calls for the placing of the pictures within a parallel band of constant height, with the centre of the band at about 1.5m (5ft) above floor level. The width of the band may be determined by the height of the largest vertical picture in the group, as shown in Figure 59, or by the combined heights of two or more horizontal pictures, and once this width is fixed, all other pictures are lined up to it, irrespective of the gaps between them. If it is expected that a large, blank wall is to be filled with pictures in this manner, it is worth lining up also the left-hand sides of the first pictures to be hung on the left, and completing the display later by lining up the right-hand edges of the final pictures to be hung.

The second method (see Figure 60) is known as 'constant spacing', in which the pictures are placed randomly, but always at an equal distance apart, typically 5 to 10cm (2 to 4in), irrespective of their sizes. Here, a display can grow across a wall as pictures are added, always at a constant distance apart, again with an average centre height of 1.5m (5ft), and this form of display is particularly well-suited to pictures related in subject or composition.

Stairwells call, of course, for matched sets of drawings or prints, in singles or in horizontal pairs, stepped down at the angle of the staircase (see Figure 61), while matched sets in other places look happy in constant-spacing rectangular blocks (see Figure 62).

Outside the home, the walls of waiting rooms, restaurants, halls and lobbies, canteens and offices can be brought to life with pictures, and here there is space galore to play with their grouping.

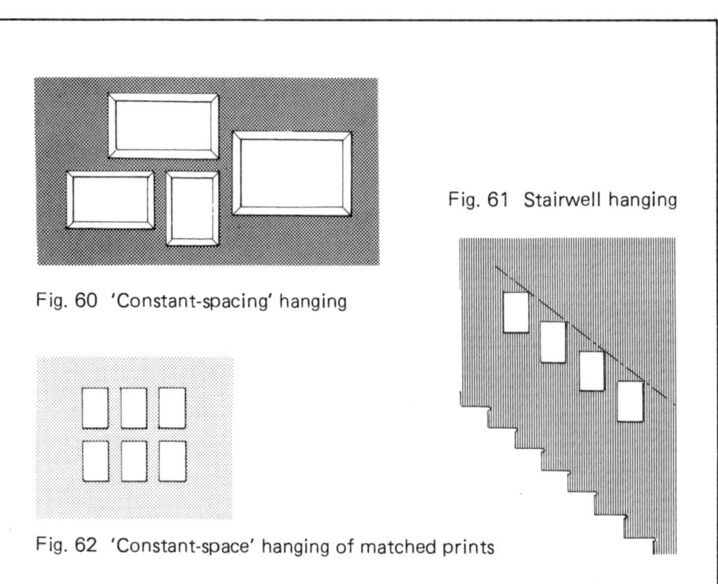

Fig. 60 'Constant-spacing' hanging

Fig. 61 Stairwell hanging

Fig. 62 'Constant-space' hanging of matched prints

Picture Hanging

Picture Cord

The most common way of hanging a picture is to thread cord through the hanging eyes and to loop the cord over a nail or a hook on the wall, but this apparently simple process can be full of pitfalls and dangers.

First, there is the matter of cord elasticity or 'stretchability'. **It is essential to have elasticity in cord or rope that is going to take shock loads, but this does not apply to picture hanging, where elasticity has a distinct disadvantage, in that it allows the picture to 'spring' on its mounting, so making it impossible to place it accurately. Further, elasticity in a cord allows 'creep', a slow but distinct stretching under load so that, as time passes, the picture slowly sinks from its original position.** Elasticity is one of the characteristics of nylon and polyester woven cords found in most hardware shops, which makes them unsuitable for picture hanging. Equally unsuitable, of course, are old bits of parcel string that are sometimes used to hang pictures.

The correct cord to use is braided cotton, often known as 'blind cord' or 'place cord', which does not stretch under correct loading. Correct loading, or 'safe loading', is a matter of cord diameter, and the table below shows the safe loads that may be put on to braided cotton cords of typical sizes. The breaking load of the cord is, of course, much higher than the safe load.

CORD DIAMETER		SAFE LOAD	
mm	in	kg	lb
2	$\frac{3}{32}$	2.5	6
3	$\frac{1}{8}$	4.5	10
4	$\frac{5}{32}$	7	15

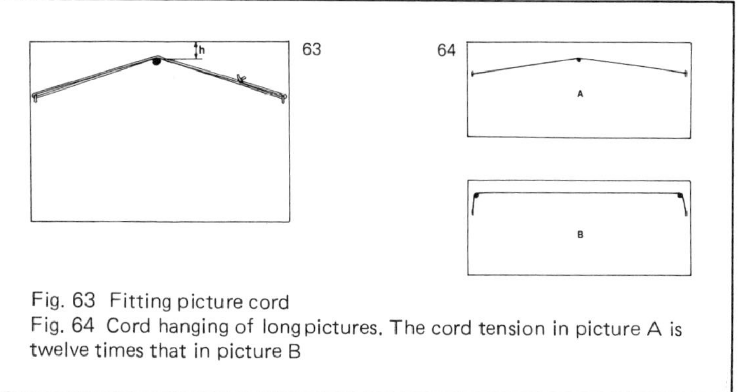

Fig. 63 Fitting picture cord
Fig. 64 Cord hanging of long pictures. The cord tension in picture A is twelve times that in picture B

The load on the cord depends on the way in which the picture is hung – the load is not the weight of the picture. Figure 63 shows the normal way of fitting a cord so that, when the picture is hung, the hook remains out of sight behind the picture. But now look at Figure 64A, which shows the same technique applied to a long, heavy picture that weighs, say, 4.5 kg (10 lb). Because of the very flat angle taken up by the stretched cord, the tension in it is six times the weight of the picture – 27 kg (60 lb)! None of the cords in the table above will take that load safely, nor will the hanging eyes, which will simply pull out of the frame.

The safe way of hanging a long, heavy picture of this nature is to use two hooks, spaced as shown in Figure 64B so that the ends of the cord are nearly vertical. The load in the cord then drops to half the weight of the picture – 2 kg (5 lb)!

The same situation of very high load applies equally to a short picture, such as that shown in Figure 63, if the cord is drawn too tight initially. It should be left slack enough to take up the steepest possible angle when taut, while still ensuring that the hook remains out of sight, behind the picture. Typically, with the hanging eyes placed one third of

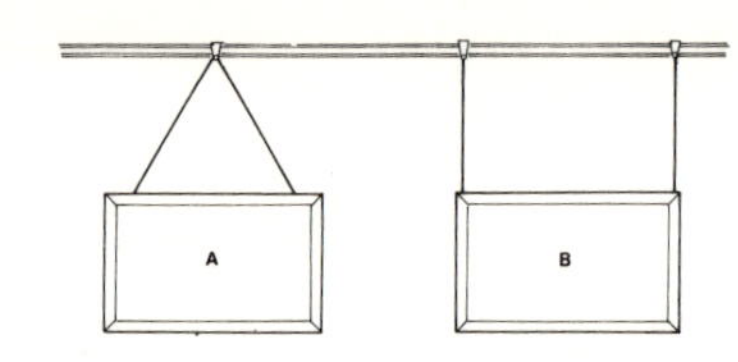

Fig. 65 Picture-rail hanging. B is preferable to A

the way down the sides of the frame, the resulting cord angle gives a load in the cord of roughly three times the weight of the picture. This can be halved immediately by doubling the cord as shown in the drawing, resulting in a final cord tension of 1.5 times the picture weight. Thus, matching the cord-strength table above with the table of picture weights and eye sizes shown on page 66, we can find the cord sizes to use on different pictures, as shown in the table below.

PICTURE SIZE (cm)	CORD DIAMETER (mm)
90 x 75	4–5
75 x 60	4
60 x 37	3
30 x 15	2

If a picture rail exists in the room (see Figure 65) the load on the cord is reduced significantly, because of the steep angle that can be attained. It is even better, and more aesthetic, to use two cords, as in the case of picture B in Figure 65.

Picture cord can be replaced by picture wire, which is immensely stronger, with no stretch, but the wire ends have to be carefully spliced and taped up to prevent the end loops opening under load. For heavy pictures, chain is better, as described on page 86.

Positioning Cord-Hung Pictures

If a picture has to be positioned accurately, as in constant-height or constant-spacing hanging (see page

81) a difficulty that sometimes has to be overcome is the adjustment of final height. While it is easy to position the nail or hook horizontally, knowing that the picture will be centred on it, the final height of the picture is not known until it is hung.

The following procedure should be used to ensure that the height will be correct. Make a light pencil mark on the wall at the point where the centre of the top of the frame must be. (This will depend on the dimensions of the picture and its distances from other pictures or walls.) Make another light pencil mark on the picture frame top, at its centre. Stand the picture on a table, face against a wall, and gently lift it off the table by its cord, using a finger tip under the cord immediately below the centre mark on the frame. Have an assistant measure the distance between the cord and the top of the frame (height 'h' in Figure 63). At this distance down from the mark on the wall, make another mark, and there drive in the nail or the hook.

Finer adjustment of final height can be achieved by putting a height-adjustment loop into the cord (see Figure 66). The loop is left slightly loose initially, so that excess cord can be taken into the loop or be drawn out of it. When the final height is exactly right, the loop is pulled tight.

Heavy Pictures

Cord-hanging of heavy pictures, weighing more than ←

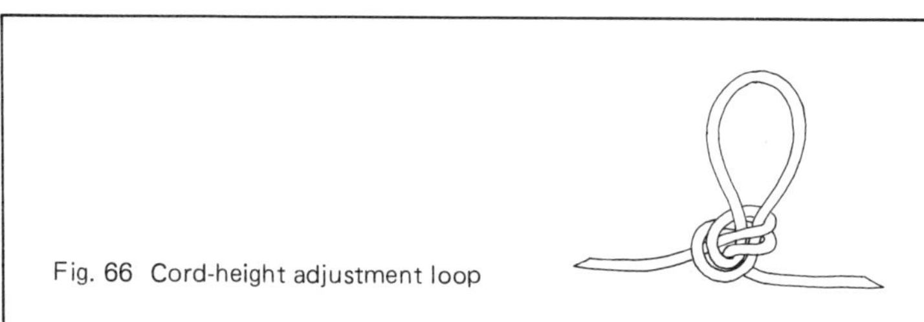

Fig. 66 Cord-height adjustment loop

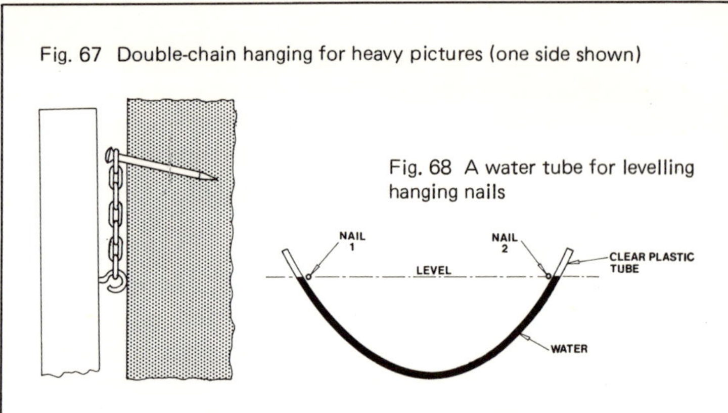

Fig. 67 Double-chain hanging for heavy pictures (one side shown)

Fig. 68 A water tube for levelling hanging nails

7 kg (15 lb), is not recommended. Double chain hanging should be used, in the manner shown in Figure 67. The hanging eyes are opened slightly to accept a link of standard 'mirror chain' or similar chain found in most hardware stores, and may be closed again for extra security. Only a few links need be fitted to each side to reach a point a few centimetres from the top of the frame, and this distance should be measured as in the preceding section.

To position the picture on the wall, draw a mark on it where the centre of the top of the frame must be. From here, measure off to the left one half of the width of the picture and deduct a couple of cm (1in). Drive in the first hook or nail here. The position of the second nail must be level with the first and the width of the picture away, less twice the original deduction (2in). If a builder's level is available, finding level is simple. If not, make your own temporary level from a piece of clear plastic tubing, filled with water, as shown in Figure 68. When hung, the picture will be level and it will never tilt.

→ **While proprietary picture hooks are good enough for smaller pictures, for chain-hanging of heavy**

pictures it is better and safer to use high-tensile masonry nails, driven deep into the wall as shown in Figure 67. For most walls, 5-cm (2-in) nails are adequate, but very soft walls might require longer nails. If the wall is made of wood, ordinary carpenter's nails will do.

Flush Hanging

Masonry nails may also be used for flush hanging of pictures, which is particularly well suited to block mounting. Figure 69 shows the method employed, in which one or two nails may be used. For a single nail, a hole of about 5mm (3/16 in) is drilled in the back of the top of the frame, exactly at the centre, taking great care, of course, not to break through at the front. The picture is then simply slipped on to a masonry nail driven in at a slight angle to the wall. A light tap with a hammer on the top of the frame (protected by a piece of wood) causes the nail head to indent slightly inside the hole, so stopping the frame from slipping forward. Two nails may be used, with holes drilled in the sides of the frame near the top, but great accuracy is required in nail driving.

With chipboard-block-mounted pictures, the hole should be drilled at least 5cm (2in) from the top of the picture to avoid tear-through of this weak material.

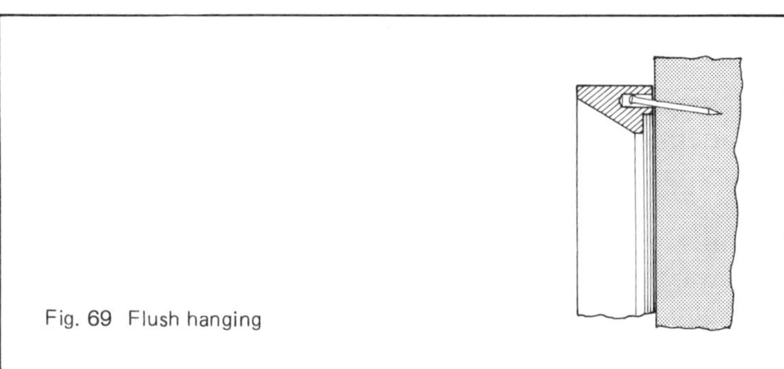

Fig. 69 Flush hanging

Hanging in Boats

None of the hanging techniques mentioned so far is suitable for boats, where pictures must be fixed rigidly to bulkheads. If access can be gained to the rear of the bulkhead, the easiest way to fix a framed picture is to place it against the bulkhead where it is to hang, mark a pair of lines down the sides of the frame, near the centre of the sides, remove the picture, drill two clearance holes inside the lines (behind the frame members), get someone to hold the picture back in place, and then go behind the bulkhead to drive a couple of wood screws into the frame from the rear.

→ **If there is no access, a modification to a metal frame can be used, as shown in Figure 70.** Here, the back of the frame, on both sides near the top, is routed or filed out to clear the head of a countersunk woodscrew that is big enough to slide inside the frame, but too big to enter without the routing. Usually, no.10 or no.12 woodscrews are suitable. Two screws are then driven into the bulkhead in the appropriate positions, leaving a fraction of the shank exposed, and the picture is slipped on to them and is pushed downwards until the screws hit the clamping plates at the top of the frame. The screws can be adjusted, in or out, to give the frame a final, tight fit to the bulkhead. A small nail, driven into the bulkhead just at the top of the frame after it is fitted, will lock it there forever.

Hanging in Galleries

Pictures in galleries are constantly on the move, as new pictures arrive and old ones depart, and there is a need for hanging systems that permit pictures to be quickly relocated without being obtrusive. Several proprietary systems exist, one of which is shown in Figure 71. This uses square-section rod, which can be slid along a channel fixed high on the wall, and which carries one or more sliding blocks. Each block is fitted with a hinged hook, so designed that, when there is no load on the hook, the block can be slid up and down the rod, but when a load is applied the block locks on to the rod. Pictures can be hung on pairs of rods, with one hook engaging with each hanging eye, or on single rods, with cord-hanging on to one block. The system is attractive but expensive.

Less expensive, but not so attractive, is chain-hanging off a picture rail, as shown in Figure 72. Here lengths of mirror chain are slid along the rail

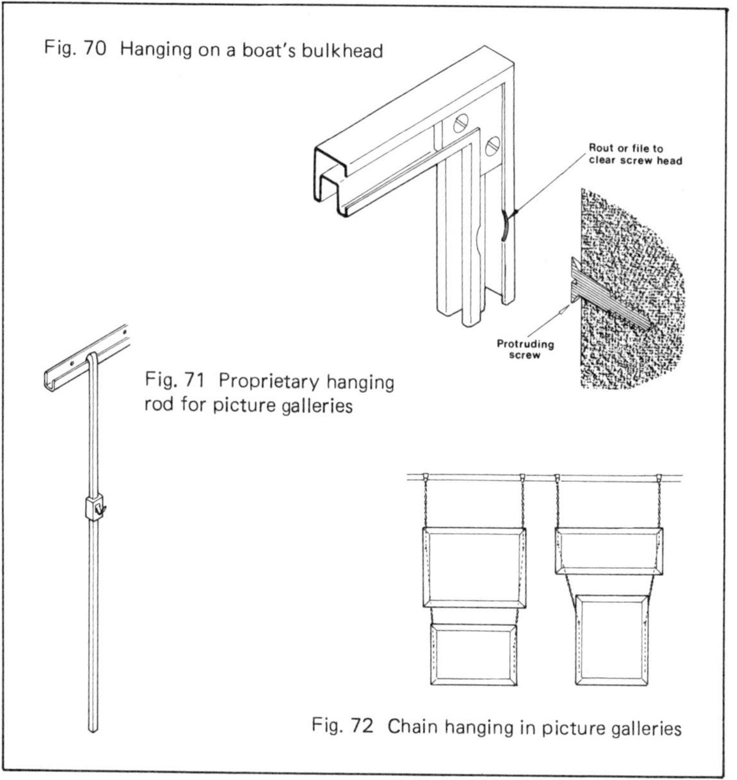

Fig. 70 Hanging on a boat's bulkhead

Fig. 71 Proprietary hanging rod for picture galleries

Fig. 72 Chain hanging in picture galleries

to suit single pictures or groups of pictures, all of which are attached to the chains by S-hooks linked to their hanging eyes.

For many light pictures, peg-board can be used, with small hanging clips let into appropriate holes, but the peg-board itself is not attractive. Covering it with hessian produces a more pleasing background, but the hessian is inevitably marred by sagging and buckling as the hanging clips pull it into the peg-board holes.

Lighting Pictures

It was mentioned earlier (page 79) that the optimum lighting for viewing pictures is diffused, even illumination covering the entire ceiling of the room, but this is reserved for very few.

In the home, ordinary house lighting is quite good enough for general picture illumination, although care has to be taken not to place pictures opposite a low, bright source of light, unless non-reflecting glass is used, or no glass at all. Occasionally, a special picture needs special lighting, and this can be accomplished by spot-lighting it. Wrong and right positions for spotlights are indicated in Figure 73, which shows

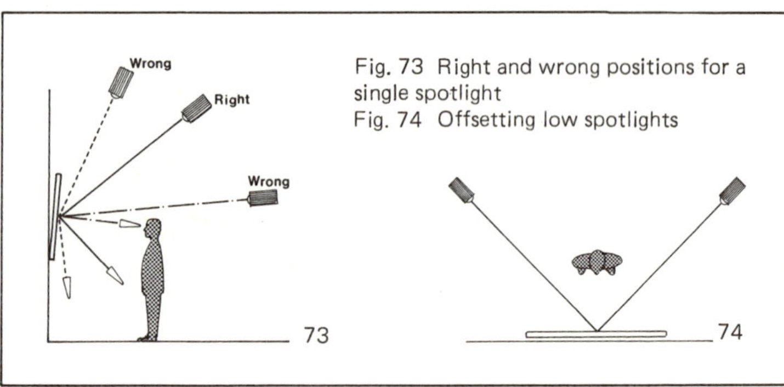

Fig. 73 Right and wrong positions for a single spotlight
Fig. 74 Offsetting low spotlights

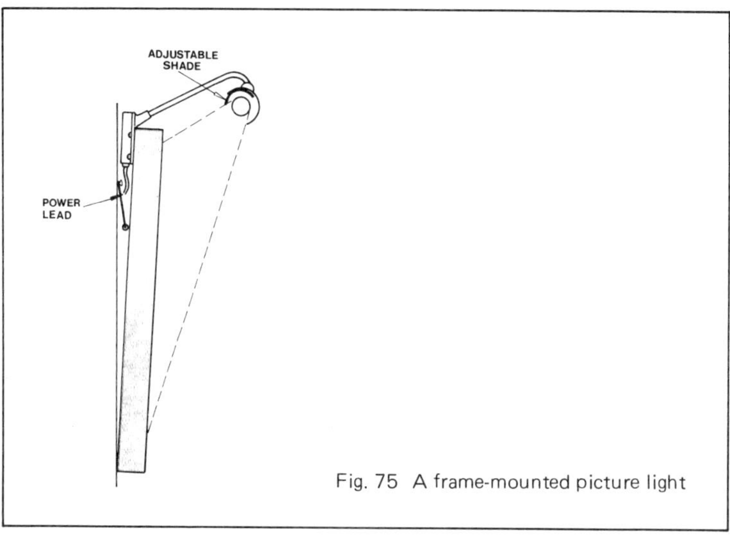

Fig. 75 A frame-mounted picture light

how too low a light will reflect straight into the viewer's eyes (even with non-reflecting glass) while too high a light will waste most of its energy on the floor. **The optimum elevation angle for a single spot is about 45°. If this height or position cannot be attained because of the room geometry, two low spots can be used instead, set out at 45° horizontally, as shown in Figure 74.** ←

Picture-mounted lights can be obtained (see Figure 75) which are fitted with adjustable heads and shades, so that the upper and lower limits of the illumination can be adjusted, quite accurately, to fall exactly within the frame. The effective width of the illumination is determined by the width of the fitting, which is normally available in three or four sizes, the illumination width being roughly four times the length of the tubular lamp. A switched and fused power outlet needs to be provided nearby.

Picture Security

The only way to ensure total security of pictures against theft is to have a complete alarm system installed, with radar movement detectors, infra-red body-heat detectors, protected windows and doors, and each picture wired into the alarm system – all very effective and very expensive.

Local alarms can, however, be fitted to individual pictures, and can make enough noise to alert the owner and frighten off the less-determined intruder. They are obtainable from certain alarm equipment suppliers, and comprise a thin box containing a battery, an electrical 'screamer' and a contact switch or a magnetic switch. The box is fixed on the wall behind the picture, and the operating switch is kept 'open' either by pressure of the picture on a contact switch, or by the presence of a magnet stuck to the back of the picture. If the picture is moved away from the wall, the operating switch closes and connects the battery to the screamer, which will go on screaming until the battery flattens or the owner turns it off with a key. Putting the picture back, or trying to open the switch again by applying pressure, will not silence the device, which has to be smashed to quieten it without a key.

Enjoy Your Pictures

If you have read your way through this book, you will probably have concluded that picture framing and hanging is somewhat more complex than you first thought. It is a mixture of aesthetics, craftsmanship and technology, all of which are brought together to make the best of a picture.

The first part of the book has shown you what the professional can do, and how you can select what suits you best from what he offers. The second part has shown you how to do it yourself, but it also draws attention to what may be best left to the professional because he has the machinery or the special tools and techniques that are sometimes required. The more you do yourself, the more you will appreciate the art of picture framing (and the technology of picture hanging), and the more you will appreciate the aesthetic pleasure that can be derived from high-quality, perfect framing.

What matters in the end is that, whether you buy your frames or make them, you are now more aware of what can be done to display your pictures in your home: pictures which otherwise might never see the light of day; pictures that you have yet to buy – or to paint; pictures that will intrigue and amuse your friends and brighten your walls; pictures sitting snugly and safely in their well-made homes; pictures for you to enjoy.

Index